MW00611434

# SELL
### with
# SWAGGER

# SELL

## with

# SWAGGER

## The Quick-Hit Guide
## to Crushing Your Quota

Timothy A. Zielinski

**LIONCREST**
PUBLISHING

Copyright © 2022 Timothy A. Zielinski

*All rights reserved.*

**SELL with SWAGGER**

*The Quick-Hit Guide to Crushing Your Quota*

ISBN  978-1-5445-3312-4  *Hardcover*
      978-1-5445-3313-1  *Paperback*
      978-1-5445-3314-8  *Ebook*

# Contents

# Introduction

Would you like to know what *real* swagger is when it comes to sales?

It's not about being suave and debonair—it's about projecting confidence. It's knowing you'll crush your quota every time. Knowing that *you've got this!* It's when you *know that you know that you know.* It's like Neo at the end of *The Matrix* movie blocking every punch with one hand while barely paying attention.

It's being like Michael Jordan. Before he won six NBA Championships and became universally known, people who didn't even know him at the time said there was something about his presence when he walked into a room. He carried himself a certain way and gave off a certain vibe.

**Real swagger is *mastering your craft.***

To become a master at anything takes time and discipline, so mastering your sales game is no different. However, this book will fast-track you through the time and discipline requirements because it maps out all of the sales-mastering components for you. I had to figure out all of these components on my own, so I condensed them into bite-sized chunks for you.

Nearly everything you need to know about mastering sales can be sorted into three categories: mindset, grindset, and skillset.

When you work in sales, you already have the odds stacked against you because of stereotypes like "the cheesy salesman" or "the con artist." So you immediately have to overcome this obstacle by showcasing your knowledge and expertise in your specific area of sales.

When you become a master of your craft, you don't have to fake anything or try to be a smooth talker, because you'll actually know what you're talking about. You'll naturally be more confident in your interactions with potential clients.

Now, to be clear, I'm not undermining the craft of persuasion or having a charming personality, but I've never been gifted in those areas. I had to discover what other variables were at play between a salesperson and a sale.

**Real swagger is *knowing your numbers.***

I've always been a math guy, so tracking numbers and crunching data to see how I could fine-tune my sales game just made sense to me.

Every salesperson has a quota, number, or goal that they have to reach. However, too many salespeople either barely hit their quota or don't hit it at all. Year after year, they continue to work hard and they barely make it. Meanwhile, they might see other sales reps in their company or industry reaching 200 percent of their quota and receiving giant commission checks. Yet somehow it doesn't seem like those sales reps are working any harder.

I bet you've heard the saying, "Work smarter, not harder," right? It's a pretty simple concept to understand in terms of input vs. output or time vs. money. When you work in sales, you don't get paid based on the number of hours you clocked or how much effort you put in—you get paid based on your results.

But at the end of the day, salespeople usually default to just working more and more hours because it's the only thing they know how to do.

If your approach to sales isn't getting you the results you want, why would you keep replicating it over and over again by simply working more and more hours? It seems obvious, but that's what most people do. However, there is a better way.

Everyone has the same number of hours in the day, right? If you don't manage your time around what's effective and what gets results, how do you expect to put more money in your pocket?

I've learned that most people working in sales don't actually know what's effective and what's not. They don't know how to work smarter because they don't understand where their results come from—and that's the major problem.

But like I said, I'm a math guy, so I solved this problem. I wanted to get the most results from the efforts I put in without working myself to exhaustion. And this book will teach you how to solve it, too.

**Real swagger is** *adding value.*

Most salespeople tend to be like a concierge. They're just sitting there kind of waiting to fulfill client requests. They're really not providing a lot of value.

What I've found is that my clients like working with me because I'm not just a concierge servicing their requests. I'm actually bringing them new ideas or I'm giving them insights that will help them be more successful or help their companies be more successful.

They begin to see me less as a salesperson and more like a consultant or advisor, somebody they would pay a lot of money for advice and direction. And this factor changes the relationship. They no longer see me as someone trying to boost his commission check so he can take his wife on a trip to Europe or buy a new car. When you truly provide value, the stigma of sales instantly vanishes.

Acting like a consultant or trusted advisor rather than a concierge drastically shifts the dynamic between client and salesperson.

Of course, you may have to do a little extra work at first in order to reach a certain level of expertise in your specific area of sales, but once you feel like you know more than the client—and actually believe it within yourself—you'll act like it, too.

I think some salespeople hear this stuff and just say, "Okay, I don't need to be a concierge. I need to be more of a trusted advisor." But they don't really believe it in their head and heart.

If you want to be successful in sales, you need to sharpen your approach. Essentially, you need to showcase the value you bring as a sales rep.

# How I Got Here

When I started my career in sales, I didn't have any formal training or previous experience. I had to learn everything on my own. So everything that I teach people and cover in this book is from my personal experience in outside sales and having to discover solutions to the roadblocks I faced.

I never imagined a career in sales because I was a typical math-and-science kind of guy—a true introvert. To me, salespeople were the most extreme type of extroverts. They seemed to have that magical life-of-the-party personality trait specifically designed for a career in sales. They were the naturally talkative, overly friendly, and instantly buddy-buddy type of people, and that just wasn't me at all.

I've been a natural introvert my whole life. Growing up, I was never outgoing or talkative. I was shy and usually just kept to myself because I always seemed to work better independently. Even when it came to playing sports, tennis was the sport I dove into. I played singles in tennis and loved it because it was all on me—I didn't have to work with a team or worry about anyone's effort other than my own. Plus, calling out the score is the only time you have to speak—perfect for an introvert!

Throughout my college years, I remained an introvert and just seemed to figure things out better on my own. I went to the

University of Michigan and began studying architecture because I liked the idea of designing and building things. Additionally, becoming an architect seemed like a natural career path for me since it primarily focused on individual work rather than teamwork or constant face-to-face work.

But I soon learned that to be an architect, you had to be in school for five years and usually earn a master's degree to get a good job. I didn't actually like school and wanted to be done with it as soon as possible. Plus, that industry wasn't exactly booming with job opportunities or well-paying careers. So I left the architecture program to study computer science instead. From what I heard, nearly everything involving computers was on the rise and offered highly profitable opportunities.

Earning my degree was a grind, but even before graduation, I had already signed an offer with an IT consulting company and had everything lined up to begin work. A lot of my classmates followed this same scenario. We were all thrilled and thought we were on top of the world because the tech scene was booming and had massive hype. The industry was paying top dollar for skilled computer science majors like myself, and I was ready to make a lot of money, travel, and enjoy life.

Then, right before I graduated in 2001, the dot-com bubble hit. As a result, my job offer was rescinded. Many of the rapidly growing tech companies suddenly froze and had to halt their hiring. I wound up moving back in with my parents and looking for work—my dreams were crushed.

I spent the first few years of my professional career bouncing around different jobs and companies, doing everything from website development to Java programming. After a couple years, I found myself working in tech support for an IT software and services company.

Up until this point, the thought of working in sales had never crossed my mind, but something shifted in me when I was in the tech support role. I was constantly around the sales and marketing teams, and I started developing more of an interest in the business side of things. I was intrigued by sales because these guys and gals had more autonomy and freedom, and were paid on their results. It was pretty clear to me that I needed to venture over to that side of the company.

So I did. I talked my way into an open position in product marketing, which was a pretty big leap for a programmer and tech guy like me, but I made the transition and never looked back. I just kept working my way up into different marketing positions. I spent some time in product marketing, email marketing, and digital marketing. Then, to my surprise, my path veered into sales.

I was at a company meeting where the VP of sales was giving an inspirational speech to excite the sales team. His energy had the room clapping, cheering, and fired up like they were at a motivational conference. Even though none of what he said was relevant to me or the rest of the marketing team, I couldn't help but be fired up as well. It was like a switch had gone off in my head that made me realize that I should be in sales. I should be sitting in the front rows right now with the rest of the sales team. *This is for me!*

That moment was certainly the catalyst that shifted my attention to sales. I took immediate action and started talking to my management about transitioning over to the sales team. Despite my former doubts, I made it happen and started working in sales for the very first time. My role was in inside sales where I operated on my own to close deals but also set up meetings for the outside sales team.

Starting out was difficult, as I had a lot to learn. It was a nonstop grind of phone calls and sending out emails, but I was motivated. Over time, I got better and better and soon came to master knocking down doors and getting into new accounts.

One of those outside salespeople told me that I was crushing it and opening a lot of doors for him. I was lining up sales calls with potential clients he hadn't been able to reach, helping him open new accounts, and making his job super easy.

He said, "You should think about carrying a bag."

At that time, I had no idea what he meant by that, but it was slang for working in outside sales, being on the road, and carrying a laptop and other supplies in a travel bag.

I told him I wasn't a schmoozer and had no interest in trying to flatter potential clients by taking them to lunch or meeting them for cocktails. But he kept naming all these reasons why I should consider outside sales, including the money and autonomy. He was quite a salesman, and he pretty much talked me into pursuing field-based sales. So I became a schmoozer afterall—go figure.

In 2010, after being in inside sales for three years, I finally got an offer to work in outside sales selling enterprise software.

## About This Book

All of the skills, tools, and insights you'll find on these pages are based on my learned experience from working in outside sales. In other words, I'm not writing about a bunch of theories and principles people learn in business school.

I ventured into sales because I saw a better future for myself— and I made the right choice. I make ten times more than I was making as a computer programmer. If I can do it, so can you.

If you want to know how to sell with swagger, this book is your fast-track. It identifies three disciplines that a salesperson at any level, and in any industry, can use to sharpen their sales wit and salespersona. As I mentioned earlier, these are mindset, grindset, and skillset.

Each chapter builds upon aspects of these disciplines with easy-to-implement action items to help you sharpen each of them. I offer practical and tactical hacks for the everyday sales-person to implement. However, this book isn't a magical bag of gimmicks or "get-rich-quick" promises. It will teach you what to do and how to do it, but at the end of the day, only you can put in the work.

If you're hungry for success and willing to work hard, this book will benefit you. Having the mindset to grind is exceptionally important—it's the foundation of success in sales. That's why Chapter 1 is about finding the motivational drive to fuel your fire. It's the prerequisite to the rest of the book.

Yet grinding hard isn't enough if you're channeling your energy down a rabbit hole. This book will show you how to work effec-tively in a clear direction with a specific skillset targeted for success in sales.

If you're with me, let's begin.

# Part I

# REFINE YOUR MIND

# Chapter 1

# FUEL YOUR FIRE

Do you know how to put your socks on?

The legendary UCLA men's basketball coach, John Wooden, began the very first practice of each new season by sitting his team down and explaining the proper way to put on socks. Coach Wooden was one of the greatest coaches of all time, leading his teams to ten NCAA titles in twelve seasons. Each year his new players were eager to hear his coaching secrets, not how to put on their socks.

He covered minute details about the heel of the sock fitting snug with no wrinkles or slack extending all the way to the toes. He would then demonstrate—literally *demonstrate*—how to put on socks and shoes and how to lace them up properly.

He wasn't speaking in metaphors or trying to be funny; he was legitimately serious about every single player on his team wearing socks and shoes correctly. He explained that bunched-up socks or loosely tied shoes create blisters, and if you develop blisters, you're either going to miss a practice or not perform at your best. For John Wooden, properly fitted socks and shoes were the prerequisites for basketball players to sustain their daily performance.

Likewise, this chapter covers the prerequisites for a salesperson to sustain their daily performance.

You can't overlook the basics and expect everything else to just fall in place. If your primary focus is to work as hard as possible to meet your quota, maybe you will and maybe you won't, but you'll likely burn yourself out. However, applying a few baseline tactics will help you blast through your quota every single time.

**SWAGGER TIP:** Identify and master the basics of your job.

If you're serious about achieving phenomenal results in sales, you need to fuel your own fire. This is the very basic "put your socks on" foundation for a salesperson. This book is filled with a ton of tips, takeaways, and easy-to-implement hacks—but these are the building blocks of selling with swagger, and these building blocks won't fit together if you don't have some of the basics down first.

Think of it this way—you can stack a bunch of bricks together and say you're building a house, but that structure will never be a house without cement in between the bricks to hold them together. The concepts in this chapter are the cement you need to make everything fit together, work together, and hold together.

If you choose to breeze past these concepts because it sounds too simple or even hoity-toity, you'll be setting yourself up for something to come along and derail your entire mission.

Salespeople have different levels of personal skills, business skills, selling skills, productivity skills, and everything else. However, I've learned that salespeople often neglect working on the most basic skills that are easy to learn, sharpen, and master. These basic skills often have the most impact on your success.

If you truly have a relentless mindset to excel in sales, an enhanced skillset will follow because you'll keep pushing yourself to learn, improve, and sharpen every aspect of your sales game.

Knowing how to fuel your fire, and working relentlessly to do so, is how you start working your way up to a level playing field and then continue to soar on past it. I'm primarily referring to actively seeking out new strategies and ideas.

I found a connection that situated me in a unique selling position: my background was in writing software and now I'm selling software.

I had a desire to learn everything because I was hungry. I didn't want to drag out this phase of my work life any further than I had to. I wanted to fast forward to when everything seems smooth and easy because I had learned how to operate in the sales industry. But I realized that everything was up to me.

I know that my sales methods are an achievable skillset for anyone to learn from scratch if they're hungry enough. Everything that I implemented and fine-tuned is a completely repeatable process. I follow the same methods, year after year, and they haven't failed me yet. I also teach workshops and training sessions to new hires at my company—so I've seen that plenty of other salespeople experience the same benefits.

Nobody gave me a repeatable, proven, step-by-step formula to be successful in sales.

When I moved from Detroit to Cleveland to start my first field-based sales job, I was moving my family to a new city to begin a new job that I had very little experience in. To make matters worse, the Cleveland-based sales position I had just filled had been vacant for six months, so there was very little activity going on. So of course I was uber-super-excited about this job because, as everyone knows, Cleveland is known as the Silicon Valley of the Midwest!

Like most field-based sales positions, I wasn't heading into an office each morning to collaborate with a team or be around other sales reps. I had limited guidance and quickly realized that I had a lot of logistics to figure out on my own if I wanted to avoid epic failure.

As a computer programmer, I'd spent the majority of my career in isolation and in a cerebral state writing endless lines of code. Leaping into sales was the complete opposite end of the spectrum because of the emphasis on personal interaction. I didn't have the gift of gab or that "life of the party" charisma, so simply overcoming my natural tendency to make eye contact with my shoes during a one-on-one conversation required some unlearning.

To say I had a rough start during my first year is an understatement. I inherited three unhappy customers and one deal opportunity. I was excited about this opportunity because the client had visited our headquarters and met with our executives. I was quickly deflated when they told me they decided to purchase our competitor's product. I ended that first year hitting 27 percent of my ramped quota. It was a real bummer, to say the least.

My second year wasn't much better. I only hit 59 percent of my quota. However, I was putting the work in each and every day, so I was beginning to notice a few trends and started to pay closer attention to my metrics. I kept grinding all the way through my third year and finally saw my persistence pay off— I hit 215 percent of my quota.

It wasn't a fluke. In my fourth year, my quota increased from $1.6 million to $2.1 million, but I still ended up hitting 205 percent of my quota!

My fifth and sixth years followed this trend, and my results for those years ended up at 214 percent and then 249 percent. In that sixth year, my Cleveland territory was actually the number one revenue-generating territory for the entire company worldwide. Little Cleveland, Ohio! Can you believe it?

So how did I do it?

How did a nerdy, math-and-science guy like me transition from writing software to selling software with such an uncanny rate of success?

Hard work? Well, yes, it was certainly hard work, but that analysis is too vague and doesn't carry any real meaning. Anyone can put in hard work if they have a checklist, or at least know what actions to take. But in my situation, I couldn't just start grinding away because I barely knew where to begin. My options were either *learn fast* or *fail*.

I had to fuel my own fire. I had to find the drive within myself to grind through my nine-to-five every day. I call this first discipline "Be Hungry."

I then dedicated my "after hours," or time outside of prime-time selling hours, to self-guided learning and personal development. I call this second discipline "Sharpen Your Saw."

The third discipline is simply to "Have Fun," and I don't include this notion as a freebie or something that should be dismissed. You'll be surprised at how even small doses of humor, laughter, and joy throughout your day can increase your mental stamina.

## BE HUNGRY

You need to have something bigger than your present state that will propel you through the low points. Nobody is going to be successful without working hard; that is a must. But why do people work hard? They always have a reason—something that motivates them.

Sales is a tough career of peaks and valleys. The peaks are the high points, the wins, the victories. The valleys are the low points, the "no's" and rejections. The truth is we have more valleys than peaks in sales, so you need a big vision or big dream that will propel you out of the valleys.

If you aren't truly hungry for success, you'll have a hard time reaching it.

Being hungry is a mindset that translates to physical energy—seriously. It helps you wake up energized and excited to take on the day. There's not a single person who would rather drag out their day, work more hours but be less productive, and not have any free time.

Instead, you need to identify a future state for yourself and be hungry to reach it. Think of it in terms of a goal or a milestone, but let me nuance this idea a little bit further. What you're identifying is a superior circumstance you want to arrive at in life. And being hungry is what propels you forward, over each and every roadblock, until you arrive there.

You might motivate yourself with something like a vacation or new car for hitting a goal you've set. For example, even after I experienced some success in my new sales career, I continued to drive my same run-down Oldsmobile Alero. It had a nice two-tone color, rust and dark green with a gold pinstripe on the side (chick magnet!). It was an old used car that I bought because, well, I didn't have enough money to afford a nice car. The driver's side power window got stuck one time, and then it wouldn't go up all the way. It actually got stuck in the down position, which is brutal in the cold Cleveland winter. I jerry-rigged a coat hanger under the window, which held it in the up position but didn't look right. I wanted to get it fixed, but why? It was motivating me every day, and making me hungry to get better and achieve more in sales so I could buy a nicer car.

When you have drive or hunger, your focus naturally shifts towards achieving a certain objective, and as a result, it blocks out the negative chatter, brain fog, or whatever it is that's bringing you down.

## QUICK-HIT ACTION

Determine a future state or goal that motivates you every day.

## SHARPEN YOUR SAW

Lumberjack and Lumberjohn go into the forest to saw down trees.

They both start working at 8 a.m.

Lumberjack stops for 10 minutes each hour to sharpen his saw.

Lumberjohn does not take the time to sharpen his saw.

They both end their workday at 5 p.m.

Who cut down more trees?

Even though Lumberjohn spent more time sawing, Lumberjack cut down more trees because he took the time to sharpen his tool. He took the time to be more effective at his job.

Sharpening your saw in sales is about challenging yourself to improve—and you accomplish this from being a continual learner. You need to be in competition with yourself every day and strive to beat the guy or gal who you were when you woke up.

During prime-time selling hours (7:30 a.m. to 5:30 p.m.), I'm very adamant about focusing on my workday agenda and nothing else, but outside of that timeframe, I'm always pursuing additional learning content. I started doing this in my earlier sales days when I knew I had a lot of catching up to do—and then I just never stopped.

Why would I stop sharpening my saw now? It's worked wonders for me so far.

I've read a ton of sales, business, and personal development books over the last twenty years, but I'm still always looking for the next one to pick up so I can explore fresh material and find the next great idea to implement. I'm a huge supporter of reading with a pen handy so you can mark sections to come back to or take margin notes. Often, I'll even send myself reminder notes via email just so I know I'll always be able to find them in my archives.

You don't have to go crazy and stress yourself about learning new things. Just be sure you're always working on yourself and getting better. I mainly listen to podcasts during my commutes and find it's a great way to generate new ideas that you can then go research or work on further. There are literally thousands of free podcasts and e-books that anyone can start listening to during their commuting time.

During company sales meetings, I wasn't in the back row goofing off with a coworker—I was in the front with a pen and notepad ready to learn. I would tell myself that "I'm the hungriest person in the room."

One learning tactic that a lot of salespeople disregard is role-playing to prepare for important meetings. In sports, athletes practice a lot before a big game. In sales, we often go into important meetings with very little practice. We just sort of "wing it."

Find a coworker to practice role-plays regularly. I know it's a little weird, but this is how you get better. Another good approach is to record yourself, and then listen to it and analyze it.

If you want to get ahead in sales, then take the time to sharpen your saw. Be a sponge and be hungry to learn as much as you can to fine-tune your sales game.

Set a realistic, self-learning goal for yourself. Don't commit to an hour a day if you know you don't have time for it. If this is something brand new for you, I would recommend starting with fifteen minutes a day of self-study, and then building up from there. Identify some areas where you can improve, and then seek out content to help you in those areas.

## QUICK-HIT ACTION

 Dedicate fifteen minutes of your day to self-improvement.

# MAKE IT FUN

You don't want your workday to be a tedious grind each and every day. You've got to add some fun and humor to your routine.

Multiple studies have shown that laughter is beneficial to one's personal health and well-being, so it only makes sense to add a little humor to your routine.

I lead a team conference call biweekly, and I start out each call with a joke because laughter improves your mental health. So do yourself a favor and just be sure to laugh every day—even if there's nothing to laugh at! In fact, try it right now. Do a real, deep-down belly laugh for ten seconds and try to be in a bad mood. It's not possible! You can't do it!

Would you like to know another secret about laughter? People learn best when they're laughing.

When I'm giving a demo presentation in front of a group of people, sometimes the Wi-Fi lags or my computer might be slow. But I've learned to have a little bit of fun with this scenario—I pull out this old hand crank, pretend to connect it to my laptop, and begin spinning it like it's going to solve the Wi-Fi issue. I'll casually say something like, "Sorry folks, my computer is a little old; a couple turns of the crank should get it back going. We'll be back on track in no time!"

By the time the laughter dies down, the Wi-Fi is functioning properly again and the group has been recharged.

I've also used humor to ease the tension when dealing with irritated customers. I'm sure you've heard the phrase "comic relief" before, so let's just say that I've been known to kick comic relief up a few notches in a few circumstances. One time, I had a large automotive customer that kept getting upset with me because, as they claimed, my company's software didn't work as advertised. "It's full of bugs! There's bugs everywhere," they said.

I scheduled an on-site meeting with them and arrived dressed as a bug exterminator. They were a bit confused, but I of course was anticipating that and told them that I had come to "eliminate the software bugs" they were experiencing. I actually had a pump and moved around the room like I was finding bugs and killing them! Everyone laughed, the tension instantly lightened, and the mood in a very tense situation shifted. This helped us all work together collaboratively as we addressed the challenges.

You need to have fun in your day or it's going to be a grind and you're going to come off as an abrasive salesperson. When it's natural, it radiates and puts customers at ease. You'll be invited back.

Many people you are selling to don't have fun work environments. If you are that fun person who makes them smile and laugh, they will want to be around you. They will invite you back.

I'm frequently looking for funny memes, photos, jokes, and animated GIFs.

## QUICK-HIT ACTION

 Add creative humor to your workday
and client interactions.

We've covered the basics you need to understand first—the cement you need to hold all of your bricks together. The next chapter will help you begin gathering some of the bricks you need to build a solid foundation. Your time is finite, so let's get into how to maximize your productivity.

# Chapter 2

# MAXIMIZE YOUR OUTPUT

Picture a million-dollar, thoroughbred racehorse at the Kentucky Derby. Shiny coat—healthy stature—calm and collected demeanor—explosive energy.

A championship racehorse has a team of expert trainers planning out its perfect diet, exact sleep and rest schedule, and of course, everything about its training routine that keeps it in premier physical and mental condition.

Do you know why a racehorse gets this kind of meticulous attention and care? Because a lot of money is on the line. It has to perform at peak levels exactly when it needs to.

Well, as a salesperson, you have a lot of money on the line, too, so you need to take your game seriously. During your workday, you want to perform at peak levels, to get the most productivity out of the hours you work. You want to be focused and perform at peak levels at every window of opportunity.

**SWAGGER TIP:** Treat yourself like a million-dollar salesperson and you'll become one.

It's easy to fall into bad habits that drag out your workday and/or extend your workweek into the weekend. Too many successful salespeople just work a lot of hours. They think, *if I work two times more hours than everyone else, I will achieve more.* That isn't always the case. Research studies have shown that most people have four to six hours of true, focused effort within them each day. After that amount of time, productivity declines quickly.

You shouldn't be working ten to twelve hours a day as a salesperson, especially if you're in charge of your own schedule. If you think about it, you actually create more work for yourself when you just keep working–working–working nonstop because you don't think as clearly and tasks take much longer to complete. The problem that quickly follows is the archnemesis of success: burnout. Unfortunately, salespeople are like moths to a flame when it comes to burnout.

Instead of increasing the amount of hours you work, increase the quality of each hour you work. This starts with being intentional. Are you being intentional with the hours you put in? Do you know what you want to accomplish before each workday? Don't start your workday by handling whatever tasks pop up first. Be intentional about each thing you do.

I'm a huge advocate of self-discipline, but I've realized that if someone isn't very self-disciplined, telling them to be more disciplined isn't a solution. Productivity is another one of those words people like to throw around when talking about work output. If productivity was just an on/off switch, wouldn't everyone choose to turn it on? My point is that these buzzwords have actions associated with them that aren't usually taught or explained.

We all know the busy guy or gal who runs around like a chicken with his head cut off... but how much does that guy accomplish? They are busy and very active, but being busy doesn't guarantee success. You have to be busy with the things that matter.

Don't mistake a caffeine buzz for productivity.

Be aware, the pitfall attached to productivity is functioning like a workhorse, not a racehorse. The productive mindset is attractive because everyone wants to get things done, but it's easy to focus on all of the menial tasks that don't really move the needle towards closing a deal. Understand that productivity isn't a feeling—it's about efficiency.

There's a distance to overcome between two points: $0 and your quota. And what's the shortest distance between any two points? A straight line, of course. So think of efficiency as a straight line.

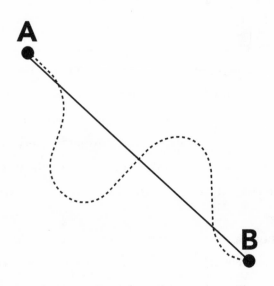

Point A is the person you are today. Point B is the salesperson you want to be—equipped with the skills, knowledge, and swagger you need to be successful in sales. Both lines represent a different path you can take to get from Point A to Point B. The dashed line is the "trial and error" method you could take to figure everything out on your own. But I've already taken that path, which is why I'm writing this book and sharing all of my sales swagger with you. The skills in this book are the straight line because they are geared towards crushing your quota—and if you want to crush your quota, you have to be efficient with your time and energy!

It doesn't matter how many actions it takes you to reach your quota—it's more about taking the right actions. So if you really want to crush your quota, you need to focus on efficiency. Call it "productivity" if you'd like, but just don't trick yourself by operating like a workhorse and then think you're being productive. Know what actions move the needle and what actions don't count for much of anything.

Everything you're doing should be effective to some degree. However, a number of factors can make sales a frustrating gig for most salespeople, because you're dealing with people directly, emotionally, and monetarily. Sometimes you're just not going to close a certain sale, no matter what you do, and neither would any other salesperson, because the person or business you're dealing with isn't able to spend the money or isn't willing to spend the money.

On the individual level, a component of mental and physical stamina is needed to keep up the pace in order to be productive each workday. I'm talking about some of the basic factors of general well-being, such as proper diet, sleep, and exercise. Don't ignore the basics of your personal wellness. Even in sales, these basics play more of a role than you think when it comes to sustaining efficiency and long-term success.

I'm not going to tell you how many hours you need to sleep each night or what your diet or workout routine should be because I'm not your doctor. But if you're constantly tired during the day, you should listen to that signal and try to figure out what's raising the alarm. What's slowing you down could be something as basic as diet. You can't expect to eat fast food twice a day and not feel sluggish throughout your afternoons. It's best to optimize your diet, so you can operate on full cylinders.

My natural inclination has always been to outwork everyone around me. And for most of my life, this meant working harder and longer than everyone else. When I was in inside sales, I was tracked on "busy" metrics like how many dials I did per day, how many emails I sent out, and how many total minutes I was on the phone. Every morning, we'd walk into the office with yesterday's metrics and how we ranked against each other. I always wanted to be at the top of the list, and I often was. I was busy, busy, busy racking up those numbers, but in reality, it wasn't getting me the results I wanted because I had coworkers closing way more deals than me. Eventually, I learned that outworking everyone else around me wasn't important. What was important was being busy with what tactics were effective.

When I began working in field sales, I learned that working smarter is the only way to outwork the competition around you. Optimizing my time usage, focusing on productivity, and overall trying to be like that million-dollar racehorse was key for me to becoming the company's number one sales rep within a few short years. I worked eight-hour days, I never worked on the weekends, and I used every single one of my twenty-six vacation days and ten holidays.

Treat your mind and body with care. Recharge your batteries each night, every weekend, and on your vacations.

## SCHEDULE FITNESS TIME

I've found that a workout halfway through the day is the perfect way to recharge myself for the second half of the day. My workdays are usually eight or nine hours long—sometimes longer if there's an after-work event with a coworker or client. However, a daily workout around noon forces me to get out of my office and away from my computer so I can reset both my mental and physical stamina.

When I step back into work mode for the second half of my day, I always feel refreshed, ready to go, and more productive compared to how I felt right before I left for the gym. You might think the opposite should occur—that I would be more tired after working out and burning all those calories—but that's just not how it works! I truly feel recharged and have more energy.

If you don't believe me, then try this out for yourself!

Schedule your workout slot in your calendar so nobody can book a meeting over it. Because it's that important. It's your personal time but also your physical and mental time.

I know many people work out early in the morning because that timeframe works best for them, but I find that I get a better workout if I do it near lunch or midday. Plus, I look forward to my workout because it breaks up the day and energizes me for the second half of the day. If I don't work out during midday, I end up needing an extra dose of coffee to keep me going.

I don't go crazy with my midday workout. I'm primarily trying to just get my blood pumping to help loosen up the body and clear the mind. Personally, I like to hit the cross-training weights for about 30 minutes and then follow up with 5 minutes of stretching, but do what works for you.

I work out five days a week, and four of those workouts are during the workweek. I'm only away from my desk for a total of one hour. But that one hour is so valuable to my overall work-day because sitting in front of your computer all day can get mundane—especially day after day—so an hour away from your workspace will have a positive effect on your productivity.

I understand there are busy days, even busy cycles, when you truly can't fit a workout into your schedule. But the, "I'm too-busy" excuse is too easy and will hurt you in the long run. After a workout, you'll have a clearer mind and will feel recharged to more effectively tackle your work. It will more than make up for the time you "lost" by going to the gym.

There are just so many mental and physical health benefits: lower stress levels, clearer mind, better sleep cycles, and too many more to list!

## QUICK-HIT ACTION

Prioritize exercise in your schedule
every day.

# ELIMINATE
# DISTRACTIONS

*Please silence your cell phone while reading this section.*

Take measures to minimize the interruptions around you. There's at least one or two easy items that most people can take out of the equation within a matter of seconds. If facing a window distracts you, move your desk to a different angle. Would you like to know a trick about noisy conversations and other sounds? They don't make a sound if you're wearing headphones.

Salespeople tend to bounce around a lot between menial tasks—they get things done but they don't work very intentionally or get the most important items off their plate. So keep to the task at hand. It takes your brain too long to transition back and forth in a productive manner between multiple tasks.

I mean, let's be honest, most of us in sales have ADD. Our mind is always bouncing from thing to thing. Don't allow that natural tendency to distract you from being focused on a critical task.

During prime-time work hours, I am totally focused on my work output. Anything that's not helping me move the needle towards my goal is a distraction, so I eliminate those distractions.

Once you are in the mode of getting a certain task done, follow through until you complete it. Think of that million-dollar racehorse again—it's trained to have tunnel vision on race days, and it even wears blinders to help eliminate distractions during the race. I'm not saying eliminate distractions all day, but when you're working on something important, you should definitely do that, and only that.

Email is one of the worst distractions. Don't let email dictate your day and derail you from what's important. You should set your priorities each day—not your email! If you start your day by checking email, you are letting others drive your priorities.

Email alerts are one of the biggest pitfalls when it comes to distractions. I see so many people get an alert sound when a new email arrives, or a desktop notification, and that is just on their work computer. You add in personal email alerts, alerts on their phone, and even on their Apple Watch—it's no wonder people have ADD. Turn these off!

I had a guy on my sales team who was always the first to respond to the group emails I sent out. His estimated response time was ninety seconds or less. Often, I would finish sending out a team email and would leave my desk for a moment to grab some coffee or refill my water bottle, and by the time I arrived back at my desk, I already had a reply from him.

This sounds great, right? This is exactly how you win a lot of brownie points with your sales manager and clients, right? Not really. This scenario occurred so consistently that it was pretty obvious he kept his email tab open all day, or at least his email notifications were kept on, and he stopped whatever he was working on and transitioned to his inbox every time he received a new email.

My emails were never that urgent or time pressing, so I felt compelled to address him about this matter because I wanted to help him tighten up this area of his sales game. After I talked with him for a few minutes, he reluctantly agreed to let me turn off his desktop email alerts.

"Are you sure?" I asked him because he still seemed hesitant.

"I'll give it a try," he said.

I explained further that he wasn't actually getting important work done by answering emails. He wasn't focusing on the big objectives that move the needle.

The very next day, however, he had his email alerts turned back on. For some reason, he just couldn't deal with not knowing when emails came through. I joked with him about it, but in all seriousness, this tiny, simple issue significantly hindered this salesman. He let other people and emails dictate his priorities, which is a major distraction to get the really important, big items completed.

You don't want to be someone's hamster on a wheel, just running in circles, or someone's doormat, so turn off those alerts!

From a client's perspective, if you're responding within five minutes of receiving their email—every time—imagine what their thoughts might be. *You must not be that busy. Don't you have anything else going on during your workday?* Or even, *Am I your only client?* Even if they are your only client, you definitely don't want to give that impression. Nobody wants to be the first or only client to anyone—it creates a negative connotation.

Additionally, you've set the expectations that you'll always respond immediately, so they'll get frustrated when you don't. On the reverse side, if you simply respond within a reasonable amount of time, like later that day or the next, it communicates that you're busy (which you should be if you're in sales) and that your time is important. This is actually a bigger deal than you may realize, because it's connected to your salespersona. You'll be accepted more like a trusted advisor we talked about earlier, rather than a cheesy salesperson waiting around to spring into action when you finally get the opportunity.

So turn off your email alerts and instead check your email at prearranged, scheduled times. Resist the need to consistently check your email throughout the day.

If people would turn their phone over so they don't see the alerts and turn off their work computer email alerts, most distractions would be eliminated. Try it!

## QUICK-HIT ACTION

 Eliminate all distractions when you work on important tasks.

# FIND YOUR FLOW

When is your most productive time frame? You should know the answer to this question, but if you don't, your preliminary assignment for this section is to reflect and determine what part of the twenty-four-hour day is most productive for you.

Most research studies have indicated that people are most productive in the morning, and for me, this is certainly the case. I wake up, have my morning prayer time, and then start my workday with a hot cup of coffee. For me, coffee is the signal that it's time to flip the switch to work mode.

With my mind fresh and after my morning caffeine, I tackle my most important task first thing. I like to start my day by getting into a flow state where I'm completely focused and productive on the task at hand. I imagine myself as that million-dollar racehorse with tunnel vision!

Flow is a mindset level I try to reach every single day. I think of it as a mix of tunnel vision + the daily grind + feeling good about my work pace and what I'm accomplishing. The amount of work I'm capable of getting done each day often depends on how quickly I find my flow state and how long I'm able to maintain it.

Whether the morning is already your most productive time, or you're looking to get into the routine of making it your most productive time, the first objective you should focus on implementing is scheduling a sixty- to ninety-minute focus session for yourself first thing in the morning. Don't open your email or work on something light and easy. Instead, dive right into one of the biggest tasks on your agenda and try to blast through it in an hour. Be sure to give yourself a ten- to fifteen-minute break immediately following your focus session—because your brain and mental stamina will need it if you're doing this right!

The goal of your focus session is to get into your flow early, starting with the very first task you begin, and then continue to use the momentum you've worked up to as you transition to task after task throughout your day.

Athletes often call this tactic "getting in the zone." You've probably seen NBA players wear headphones getting off of the team bus on game days, or even while they're shooting and stretching. They're trying to block out all other distractions so they can focus on the task at hand and find their flow. Most athletes have a specific routine they go through, and maybe even some superstitious things they do as well—like wearing a lucky pair of socks or something. They do whatever it takes them to get into an enlightened state to perform at their best. We should do the same in sales!

A lot of people need their morning coffee to springboard their day forward. Other individuals might need music, meditation, or some other form of catalyst time to help boost them into flow mode. Don't think of these boosters as a crutch or negative routine you have to go through—lean into them! The overall objective is to know what it takes to find your flow and then to replicate it each day as part of your routine.

Once you get into a highly productive state, maintain it! It's much easier to grind through your day if you feel aligned and in rhythm than to grind through your day feeling stressed and rushed to get something done.

## QUICK-HIT ACTION

Begin each morning with a
focus session to accomplish your
most important tasks.

Now that you're able to maximize your output and be more productive, let's move on to prioritization. In sales, there are so many things to do! So many things that you can fill your day with. By organizing your priorities and scheduling your day, you'll increase your effectiveness. Simple, right? Maybe not . . . let's examine this closer in the next chapter.

# Chapter 3

# REGIMENT
# YOUR TIME

Time is a finite resource. Nobody can manufacture more time. We all have twenty-four hours a day. We need time to sleep, eat, sync up with family, and pay bills.

It's all about making the most out of your own, personal twenty-four-hour cycle, each and every day. A great example of this is found in the movie *Pursuit of Happyness* (if you haven't seen it, sorry, I'm going to ruin it for you).

Based on a true story, Will Smith plays Chris Gardner—someone who is truly hungry to be successful and just wants to win for himself and his family. He goes through a huge rough patch in his life, involving his wife leaving him, losing his house, going to jail, winding up on the street with his son, and sleeping in a subway bathroom.

He gets an opportunity to interview for a really good sales job, but he has to compete against roughly thirty other individuals, and only one of them will get the job. Most or all of his competition is younger than him, don't have kids, and aren't living on the street. He realizes he's at a huge disadvantage because everyone else has the ability to stay late and work more hours, which they do, while he can only be at the office between eight and five because he has to pick up his son at daycare. However, he notices the others taking extra long lunch breaks, constantly leaving their seats for coffee and water breaks, and just goofing off and procrastinating.

Eventually, he realizes something along the lines of *Okay, I can't work as many hours as my competition, but I can utilize my time better and be more effective during the hours that I do have*. The story then unfolds to display his realigned mindset and grindset: the new actions he starts to implement in order to rise to the challenge.

For example, when he's making sales calls, he doesn't put the phone down between calls. He keeps the phone up to his ear and immediately dials the next phone number on his list. He keeps this strategy up dial after dial in order to achieve as many calls as possible in his allotted time. On the other hand, his competition is ending a call, putting the phone down, repositioning their sitting position or getting up, resetting, and then dialing again.

It's a very emotional story because it takes a while for his hard work to pay off, and in the meantime, you see him and his son sleeping in the subway bathroom, trying to overcome their other struggles of being homeless. Even when they achieve a small win of getting a roof over their head by means of a homeless shelter, they don't control the room's light switch, so you see "Chris Gardner" up late at night using a flashlight to study for a major test that is soon to take place at the end of his internship.

Overall, he ends up landing the sales job he was competing for even though the cards were stacked against him. And from that point, he is able to turn his situation around to create a better life for himself and his son.

This story is a great example of being smart with your time without working more hours. Most salespeople default to working more hours, but working more hours is not the answer—it's a pitfall.

**SWAGGER TIP:** Be intentional about your day by managing your time well.

People in every profession are starting to overwork themselves more and more. Salespeople have always had a bad tendency to fall into this routine because they are "always on." However, "always on" leads to burnout faster than most people realize.

The problem is that working overtime or nonstop often feels like you're accomplishing something. It feels good because you think you're clearing your email inbox or making some headway on a project, but what you don't realize is you're never shutting off.

People like this are more than likely just operating like a workhorse.

It's critical that you have a healthy balance of work and non-work. Non-work keeps you grounded to know what you're working for. Further, non-work helps you reset your mind each day so you can wake up energized and motivated to tackle your work objectives for a predetermined time frame.

My mindset is that 7:30 a.m. to 5 p.m. is my prime time work hours. I take a one-hour break in the middle to do a workout, but other than that, my sole focus is on work. I don't want to be dealing with work late into the evening or on the weekends because that's my personal and family time.

And vice versa: I don't spend my designated work time dealing with personal or family matters. Because I'm very strict about my work-life balance, I don't sway in and out of the stress and burnout like so many salespeople tend to do.

When I'm done with my workday and workweek, I'm *completely done*. I'm not checking emails on my phone or sitting at my computer late at night trying to finish up a few things. I'm focusing on my personal agenda, like coaching my kids' soccer team or enjoying time with my family and friends.

The most beneficial part about not working in the evenings is that when the morning comes and it's time to jump back into work mode, I feel mentally refreshed and recharged to handle my workday with the same intensity that I always do. I wouldn't feel this way if I constantly worked late or didn't get to spend time with my family.

I'm just as strict about my weekend time off as I am about my evening. When I come into work on Monday, I'm excited and ready to go because I've enjoyed my time away and feel mentally refreshed and prepared to take on another workweek. Evenings are about recharging your daily battery, but the weekends are about resetting your mental stamina so you can go the five-day distance once again.

Additionally, taking vacations a few times a year is also critical to your mental well-being and energy. I am definitely more creative once I get back from a vacation. My brain is free, I can think better, and I feel inspired to solve any problems or roadblocks I was encountering before. Sometimes you just need a bit of creativity to kick things up a notch or solve a problem, like how to get your foot in the door of a major account you've had on your radar.

Here are the three most effective ways that I've found to help stay strict about my professional time so I can better enjoy my personal time.

## PLAN TOMORROW TODAY

Each workday, the last fifteen to thirty minutes of my calendar is blocked out for me to go through my end-of-day routine, which simply involves planning my agenda for the next day. This may sound like a lot of time, but you may have to go through emails, to-do lists, and prioritize everything that comes up. It might take you thirty minutes at first, but over time as you become more fluent in this routine, fifteen minutes should be your goal.

Not only does this routine allow me to close down my current workday and transition out of work mode, it allows me to hit the ground running the next day because I know exactly what my schedule is and what I need to accomplish.

When I look at tomorrow and plan it out, it puts my brain at ease. I know that everything is written down on paper and I'm not going to forget anything. I'm fully aware of what's waiting for me when I transition back into work mode the next day.

It's not rocket surgery (BTW: rocket surgery = rocket science x brain surgery)—all I do is look at the calendar for tomorrow and start by writing out the meetings and calls I have at a set time. From there, I fill in the priority objectives I know I need to accomplish—this is important—don't let priority items weigh you down all day. And finally, I build out a task list in-between to ensure I'm always working towards moving the needle.

I take the time to plan the next day. It builds your confidence to plan the day and then accomplish the day as you planned it.

Think of planning tomorrow today in terms of a mind hack or even a mental health hack. If I didn't bring closure to the workday, items would continue to linger in my head. I'd be rechecking emails on my phone all evening or constantly thinking about open cycles that I don't want to forget. However, I've found that a clean "shut down" to the workday allows me to better focus on my family and other non-work-related activities. Plus, I sleep better.

A lot of salespeople just keep working casually through the evening. If this sounds like you, I understand where you're coming from. Sales is a profession that requires so many different tasks in a day, because there's just a lot of action items to take care of. But trust me, "casually" working through the evenings is dangerous. It tricks you into being casual during your regular working hours, because you know you have all evening and night to catch up.

The habit of planning tomorrow today has been a game-changer for me, especially on Fridays, because it helps me enjoy the weekend. I bring complete closure to the week by planning for Monday, and then shut down the workweek and say, "Okay, this week's done. I'm done." I'm basically programming my brain to say, "I'm not going to work this weekend." I'm done with Friday and I have my plan for Monday. So why would I need to work over the weekend?

If you're constantly working and not enjoying your evenings, weekends, or any downtime at all, you're not setting yourself up for long-term success. You need to recharge your batteries and reset completely during the weekend.

## QUICK-HIT ACTION

 End each day with fifteen to thirty minutes of planning for the next day.

# MANAGE A TASK LIST

Don't confuse a task list with your schedule, daily objectives, or anything else along those lines. A task list is an ongoing, master to-do list that you are always adding to and deleting from. Whenever a new task pops up for the first time, add it to the master list.

Now, why would I take the time to explain a simple task list?

Do you know what happens when you don't write anything down, don't use organization tools, and don't manage a task list, but rely instead on your memory to recall anything and everything you need?

You overload your brain files! Each task you try to remember adds a tiny amount of outside stress to your mind, because you haven't "backed up" your mental files to notes on a page. So you're doomed if you don't remember everything.

Lingering tasks will cause insomnia because they are open cycles that you haven't devoted to a simple list. Even tasks a few weeks down the road will pop up randomly whenever you're trying to get some sleep, because your mind is over its capacity limit and just firing random signals.

Just get your tasks on a list so your brain can relax!

I derive many of my tasks when I check emails, but tasks can obviously come up in a variety of ways.

I recommend a digital task list because, if you're like me, you're receiving an influx of new tasks on a daily basis. Whether it's orders you need to process for clients, a request from your sales manager, or a number of other business matters—it's too easy for all of these small action items to pile up. So using a digital list allows you to shuffle things around easily, prioritize or categorize items, and set reminder notifications for specific tasks.

I use the task list in Outlook, but Gmail, iCloud, and several other email/calendar providers have nearly the same type of task list already integrated. There are also a ton of free apps if you want to explore even more options, so just find one that works for you and stick with it.

There's never a day when I can complete everything on my task list. My list is consistently lengthy, so I have several days worth of tasks spread out across time. Numerous items are listed on the backburner, such as tasks I don't need to even think about for two or three weeks. I arrange my tasks using a simple A–B–C code system to indicate priority level, which I learned from Bryan Tracy's *Eat that Frog*. Also, each task has a date that it needs to be completed by.

A-tasks are time-pressing items that I must take care of that day. I then put a number after it to prioritize it. For instance, A1 is the most important item for the day and A2 is second. On most days, A1 is "prep for tomorrow's meetings" and A2 is "follow-up on yesterday's meetings." In sales, both A1 and A2 are critical to my success, so I do them first thing in the morning because, as I mentioned earlier in "Find Your Flow," the early morning is my most productive time of the day.

B-tasks are next in priority and are items that should be handled that day if all A's are completed.

C-tasks are items of lesser priority and get worked on if all A's and B's are done. Like B's, I might take on these tasks if some meetings cancel that day. At most, I have six A-tasks scheduled per day and a lesser amount of B-tasks and C-tasks. With other meetings scattered throughout, there just isn't enough time in the day to do more than that.

Here's a general representation of what I'm talking about:

## 🏳 Tomorrow

| | | |
|---|---|---|
| ✓ | A1: prep tomorrow's meetings | Tue 12/21/2021 |
| ✓ | A2: meeting follow-ups | Tue 12/21/2021 |
| ✓ | A3: QBR setup | Tue 12/21/2021 |
| ✓ | A4: SFDC opp updates | Tue 12/21/2021 |
| ↻ | A5: plan tomorrow/do mileage | Tue 12/21/2021 |
| ✓ | B1: complete MSW training | Tue 12/21/2021 |
| ✓ | B2: promote conference | Tue 12/21/2021 |
| ✓ | WF: Mike Woodling, fu on 12/20 email | Tue 12/21/2021 |

When tasks are on standby until I hear back from someone, I'll code them with a WF to signal "waiting for." I learned this concept from one of the best books on time management: *Getting Things Done* by David Allen. In sales, we rely on so many other people; this is a great way to keep track of those important items.

Work to eliminate a certain number of tasks every day. Each evening when you "Plan Tomorrow Today," use your task list to build out your agenda. Schedule the priority tasks first thing in the morning so they're not weighing you down all day. Then, depending on how booked the rest of your day is, assign tasks to open time slots on your agenda. And remember, if you waste time during the following workday or don't stick to your schedule, you'll never get rid of these tasks.

Manage a task list to prioritize
your objectives.

# SCHEDULE
# EVERY THIRTY MINUTES

There is a certain level of regimentation you should aim for throughout your workday. Establish your eight-to-five, or whatever time frame you choose, as a baseline and stick to it. Many salespeople struggle with this baseline and never have a clear starting point and clear stopping point in mind when they begin each day. This is a major pitfall that I've brought up several times because the issues just keep unraveling the more you explore and unpack it.

There's little room for exceptions on this matter—set hard boundaries that indicate your work time.

Break down your workday into segments or time slots that, when added together, compose the day. Personally, I believe the perfect increment is thirty-minute time slots when I'm working through my day. Anything more gets to be too detailed for me—and too much detail often slows progress.

After you block-out your meetings, assign tasks to each open thirty-minute time slot. Larger tasks might take two or three time slots, and that's perfectly fine. The goal is to have a clear direction for your day so you don't end up just letting your day happen.

In the schedule below, notice the simplicity in how I write out my schedule:

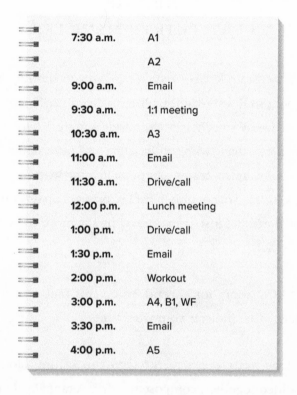

| | |
|---|---|
| **7:30 a.m.** | A1 |
| | A2 |
| **9:00 a.m.** | Email |
| **9:30 a.m.** | 1:1 meeting |
| **10:30 a.m.** | A3 |
| **11:00 a.m.** | Email |
| **11:30 a.m.** | Drive/call |
| **12:00 p.m.** | Lunch meeting |
| **1:00 p.m.** | Drive/call |
| **1:30 p.m.** | Email |
| **2:00 p.m.** | Workout |
| **3:00 p.m.** | A4, B1, WF |
| **3:30 p.m.** | Email |
| **4:00 p.m.** | A5 |

On this particular day, I had meetings at 9:30 a.m. and 12:00 p.m., so these are the first two tasks that get listed. I then proceed to assign my other tasks to an open time block until my daily schedule is fully booked. A1 and A2 tasks are priority, as I discussed in the previous section. I always take on these two tasks right away so they're not lingering over my shoulders all throughout my workday.

I have four time slots to check email, and that's the only time I check email. When checking email, I use David Allen's advice on two minutes per email, with a goal of clearing my email inbox. I read each email and spend up to two minutes on it. If it will take more than that, I schedule it for a task to be completed at a later date.

People usually have no idea how much time they end up wasting between tasks. Grabbing coffee, checking social media, or even zoning out at your desk can easily last longer than the "five minutes" you think it does. Additionally, if you don't know what task you have on your agenda next, you'll take your sweet time pondering what you should start on next. This is usually a subtle and subconscious form of procrastination.

To ensure that you're not wasting time pondering and switching tasks, schedule every thirty minutes and don't fall behind. Accomplish something that moves the needle with each time slot, but also be sure to schedule short breaks for yourself. If you know that you have a scheduled break planned in thirty minutes, you're more likely to stay on track and stick to your schedule.

It's also important to put an "end time" on a task, because this forces you to be more productive. Think about it—athletes often perform their best during the last few minutes of a game because, well, it's crunch time! Likewise, you'll also perform optimally if you give yourself a time limit on tasks and adamantly stick to that time limit.

When your thirty-minute time slot is up and it's time to move on, cross that item off your list. Continue to do this micro action every thirty minutes, because it instills confidence that you are getting things done and sticking to your agenda.

## QUICK-HIT ACTION

 Don't let your workday schedule you— schedule every thirty minutes and crush each segment.

This concludes Part I: Refine Your Mind, where we outlined some important concepts to change how you think about sales. Implementing the quick-hit actions will be internal changes that will lead to massive outward success. In Part II: Define Your Grind, we segue into building your individual sales strategy so you can continue to sustain your success and keep crushing your quota.

# Part II

# DEFINE YOUR GRIND

# Chapter 4

# SHARPEN YOUR SALESPERSONA

Almost everyone can recall stories of encounters they've had with bad salespeople. Maybe this comes easier to me because I'm in sales, and I'm an overly critical critic.

I remember the window salesman who had bad breath and loved, and I mean loved, to talk. He insisted on telling me everything about windows of which I didn't really care about. I told him to get to the point, and that I didn't need to see all of his PowerPoint slides, but he insisted. I actually started to get angry because he was wasting my time on windows that weren't pertinent to what I needed . . . and I had to endure his bad breath for much longer than I wanted. It got to the point where I didn't even want to ask him a question because every answer took five to ten minutes when a one word or one sentence response would have been sufficient. His long-winded answers made me forget what question I even asked.

I remember the lawn care sales guy who came by and told me how my lawn was in bad shape. He bent down, started picking at my grass and making unsettling faces at it. He actually interrupted me playing with my son and insulted the current lawn fertilizer I was using... big mistake! That's like calling someone's baby ugly.

We've all had these examples happen to us, and they make us distrust salespeople and usually not even like them.

Now, on the flip side, I remember a great salesperson who sold me an insect control service. He came over to my house and politely asked if we could chat. This was welcomed because I was in the middle of doing some yard work. Then he quickly introduced himself and his service and asked if I would answer a couple questions. He engaged me instead of talking to me. He quickly uncovered that we did have bugs and spiders in the house, and he mentioned how his service could solve that. Then he mentioned other houses nearby that also had just signed up for his service.

He was courteous, and he cared about helping me. And guess what? He earned my business, and I enjoyed giving it to him.

**SWAGGER TIP:** Be aware of your salespersona and the impression you make on others.

Regardless of which industry people work in, almost everyone steps into some type of persona during their workday. Consider someone who works in customer service, for example. Regardless of this person's natural personality or temperament, it's part of their job to be exceptionally friendly, helpful, and positive no matter how outraged a customer may seem.

In sales, it is beneficial to have a certain persona when interacting with clients. I'm not talking about trying to be a completely different person or trying to con anyone, I'm talking about having strong people skills and sharpening certain personality traits that are attractive to buyers. I therefore refer to a salesperson's persona as a "salespersona."

These days, buyers respond to a salespersona that is knowledgeable and helpful, not smooth and persuasive.

Once I began approaching my sales game as the "adding value" salesman, my clients and I naturally developed a relationship beyond the typical business relationship. There was a level of confidence and trust I had instilled in them, so many considered me more like a work associate or even a friend. And truly, I considered many of them friends, too.

When you reach this level, clients are thinking beyond the notion of, "Yeah, this salesperson has a great product." They actually want to reciprocate the value you've given them by continuing to give you business. They want to see you win and be successful because, first of all, you've helped them win and be successful by providing them with great products and services, and second, they feel like they're helping out a friend.

Let's look at two sides of building a sales relationship and the pitfalls attached to each side.

On the first side, some sales reps are just all relationship-driven. They constantly hit up clients with propositions like, "Hey, let's go out to lunch" or, "Hey, I've got an extra ticket to the game" or, "Hey, let's go hit some golf balls." It becomes apparent that the buddy-buddy tactic is pretty much all they know how to do when they're working towards closing a big deal. That means all of their effort is focused on building a personal relationship with clients, but little effort is spent on adding value.

On the flip side, there are salespeople who are super business-oriented. They display their value quite clearly, but they're all business—super clean-cut, super efficient with their client interactions, and super robotic on emails and calls. Although I would say value is the top priority, at the end of the day, people want to buy from people they like. Further, people would prefer to buy from a friend or fellow work associate, because that's how business works. If your friend sets up shop or opens a brewery, you do your part to support it, right?

You have to provide business value, but you also have to make yourself personable and approachable. So don't be the cool sales rep who always buys lunch, and don't be the strictly business sales rep. Learn how to balance the two with each client. Be the competent sales rep who adds value and occasionally treats his clientele to lunch, when the time is right. That's the magical combination.

The precursor to set you on this path relates back to sharpening your salespersona, especially when you're still getting to know your prospects or new customers. If you want to get better results, focus on making a friend, finding a need, and referencing success stories.

Making a friend might sound basic, but when you work in sales, it's not as simple as just being friendly. People tend to buy things emotionally, so it's important for customers to know and trust you beyond the customer/salesperson dynamic. But they're not going to make a huge company purchase if they don't have a problem that needs to be solved. So "Make a Friend" and "Find a Need" go hand in hand, but making a friend should always come first because that will make it easier to find a need.

# MAKE A FRIEND

People feel more comfortable buying something from someone they know and like, so it makes sense that inexperienced sales-people often default to, "Hey, let me treat you to lunch," early in their career. It's a quick and easy way to try to get someone to like you.

Rather than being the buddy-buddy lunch guy, I've learned that a more genuine approach to making a friend is not only easier but more effective. One of the quotes I'm always reminded of by Zig Ziglar is, "People don't care how much you know until they know how much you care."

When I'm meeting with potential customers for the first time, I have a mental list of objectives I'd like to accomplish. The initial position I take right off the bat is to make a friend.

Before I intentionally started doing this, I mainly just cared about the sale or closing the deal, and people sensed it. My inter-actions with clients weren't natural, because I was distracted by overthinking what I should say and how I should act. I was rigid. People are good at sensing other people's energy when they're putting on something of a front.

When I changed my mindset and began telling myself to be more interested in actually making a friend than just making a sale, the dynamics changed because I was more at ease. I learned to surpass the "business acquaintance" relationship with almost all of my clients and have varying degrees of friendship with many of them.

To make a friend in this type of scenario, ask conversational questions to find out what they're interested in and try to make a connection. I often use LinkedIn to learn a few talking points before I meet with someone for the first time. However, if you're in their office, look for conversational clues or cues that might point you in the right direction, like if they're a major sports fan or where they went to college.

There are a handful of universal topics that people generally enjoy talking about, like what they did over the weekend or upcoming weekend plans. Asking these types of questions allows them to share some of their interests or hobbies with you, which will almost always open the door for other questions to continue building a connection.

Bring up something about your family or kids and see if they match you with something back. If they bring up their kids, ask about them with genuine interest, their names, ages, and personalities. Most importantly, remember the names of their kids. If you don't intentionally "remember" to "remember the names," it's unlikely that you will. A few meetings later, either weeks or months down the road, bring up their kids by name and ask how they're doing. Since you cared enough to remember their kids' names, it hits them that you weren't just making small talk weeks earlier. Take note of how the business relationship prospers into a friendship from this point on, because it always happens.

Also, recognize when you're meeting with someone who is just not enjoying the "get to know you" questions. Don't keep asking question after question like a weirdo if the vibe isn't there. People are busy and many will just want to get to the point. Initially, they don't even know if you're worth their time. If this is the case, transition to the business reasons for your meeting and showcase your value right away. This dynamic occurs regularly, because people often don't care to talk to salespeople, preferring to shoo them off like a stray cat on their porch.

Strive to reach "texting level" with clientele. A texting relationship with someone means you've built a level of trust between them that could continue into a friendship. If somebody is willing to trust you with their mobile phone number, it's a good sign that you've built great rapport and trust.

I hate it when salespeople say, "The prospect went dark on me." To me, that says you weren't adamant about making a friend first, so you don't have a very good relationship with them, or you did something wrong to make them not like you.

If you make a friend first with a prospect, it's easier to stay engaged with them because they'll feel bad about "going dark on you," like they were ignoring a friend. If you don't make a friend, or worse, if they don't like you, then they won't feel bad about going dark on you.

When I have a first-time meeting, I always try to learn where people like to eat. First of all, this provides me with an excuse to reach out to them later. Secondly, it allows me to extend a meet-up invitation that is more along the lines of a friendship rather than a business meeting. I can always drop a line and say, "Hey, I'll be in the area. Do you have any lunch plans? I'd like to try that restaurant you wouldn't shut up about."

Don't try to make this a gimmick or some kind of calculated action. It's a lot easier to just genuinely care and be the guy who always makes friends.

## QUICK-HIT ACTION

Establish rapport quickly by
making a friend first.

# FIND A NEED

When someone pulls up to a car dealership and begins browsing the lot of new cars, it's usually a good indication that this
person is in the market to purchase a car. They're not going to
be surprised when a car salesperson approaches them, and in
most cases, they'll actually be anticipating it. This same person,
however, might not be so receptive to a car salesperson who is
reaching out to them by way of cold calling.

Unless someone is out shopping for something specific, no
one likes to be approached about spending their money to buy
something they hadn't planned on.

The same dynamic applies within most businesses, and this
creates one of the biggest obstacles for salespeople to navigate:
how to get a foot in the door rather than a door in the face.

Most of the prospects you reach out to aren't actively shopping
for the product/service you're selling, so they don't have a specific
"need" on their mind. Their initial response usually defaults to,
"Thanks, but we have no need for what you're selling." This type
of response doesn't open any kind of opportunity for the salesperson and doesn't extend an invitation to discuss things further.

In order to avoid the door in the face, you have to uncover a
potential need early in communication and be prepared to

showcase how and why you have the solution. This shouldn't be too far of a stretch to realize because if a prospect doesn't think they have a need/problem, then why would they want to waste time talking to a salesperson? But if you can uncover a need/problem that wasn't necessarily on the forefront of their agenda, and then provide a solution to it, you'll almost always have your foot in the door.

Keep in mind that "Make a Friend" and "Find a Need" go hand-in-hand. But making a friend must come first.

Without a need, it's unlikely the prospect will continue meeting with you. They are busy—they have work priorities—and talking to a salesperson isn't one of them.

It's important to understand that the task of finding a need is in the hands of the salesperson, not the prospect. It's only when the prospect has a critical problem that they're already aware of, something that could perhaps be detrimental to their business operation, that they would contact you for a solution. And because this is seldom the case, the salesperson must first uncover a need and present it as a problem, business threat, or other pain point.

Don't ask discovery questions like, "What keeps you up at night?" when you're trying to find a need. This is the classic and cheesy salesman question because, regardless of what the customer's response is, the salesperson will surely dive into what they have to offer and why it is the solution they need. Ask friendlier questions that show your interest in their business, plans for growth or expansion in the near future, and other questions that have a bit of depth to them. A good rule is to always ask "how" questions because they require more than a one-word response. They allow you to better understand your prospect.

Further, devise what "how" questions you plan to ask ahead of time and write them down so you can rehearse them and won't forget them. I've learned that almost all of my prospects experience the same two pain points, so I developed two "how" questions that I always ask new prospects specifically to draw out these pains.

If there's one area people and businesses *do* spend money on, it's anything and everything that can potentially make their life or job easier. So focus on the types of questions that get people talking in this direction. When you sharpen your line of questioning and pinpoint a need, you'll see this trend continue.

---

## QUICK-HIT ACTION

 Develop "how" questions that will uncover pains and problems.

# BUILD
# CREDIBILITY

From a prospect's perspective, previous success stories are so important in their decision to buy anything. Think of book reviews or product reviews online: Do you browse through a few of these before making a purchase? When shopping, have positive reviews ever led you to make a final decision and proceed to check out? These types of reviews are micro examples of customer success stories.

**Memorize a quick-reference list of customers' names.** I have a list of ten strong success stories that I can pull from and present anytime I need to. Essentially, this list is built to "name drop" other relevant companies that are using my products or services, because I want prospects to feel like "everyone" in their industry is using the software I'm selling. I have this list memorized so I can rattle off a handful of names casually and without hesitation whenever the opportunity presents itself.

Sometimes it's better to talk more in-depth about one of the success stories on your list, so you should also know some of the details about each of these customers' successes. If you're able to unpack a customer story like a "case study" to portray exactly how your product helped them, that's a huge boost in credibility.

**Tell stories for credibility.** In sales, telling stories can boost your credibility because you're showcasing the previous success a company has already experienced in using your product or service. Nearly every salesperson is going to put what they're selling on a pedestal and speak highly of it, but it's too easy for this approach to fall short in closing a sale because, frankly, people expect a salesperson to praise whatever it is that they're selling.

Instead of describing everything "about" your product, change the *way* you respond by simply tying in a customer story to relay the same information. For example, look at this statement: "The installation process is super easy. It should only take about five to ten minutes to complete." There's nothing blatantly wrong with this sentence, but it's a standard answer that reflects an easy process "in theory."

Now, look at this second example to see how you can deliver the exact same information but with more credibility: "The installation process is super easy. In fact, just last Tuesday I walked through it with *Company A*. Their environment is very similar to yours, and the entire process only took eight minutes." Do you see how this second example resonates better because you're describing a situation that actually happened?

If you don't use stories, much of what you say will come across as opinionated talk. Prospects don't want to hear a salesperson's opinion—trust me! Naturally, they'll think, "It's jaded!" So storytelling is generally just a much more beneficial approach to lean on, especially when they're used to answering client questions.

**Answering questions with a customer story.** Once again, you're simply changing the *way* you respond to customers in certain scenarios. When a customer targets a specific problem/solution, here's an example of how you might answer with a customer story: "*Company A* had that exact same problem last year before they became one of our customers. However, they eliminated this issue right away by implementing this product/service."

The more specific references you use, the more relatable and credible the story is. If you don't use a customer story, then your answers will probably sound more opinionated. They won't have as much credibility because you're the salesperson!

---

## QUICK-HIT ACTION

 Memorize and utilize your customer success stories.

---

You've completed a lot of the prep work on yourself with this chapter, so now it's time to build a strategic game plan to get after your accounts. The next chapter will help you examine the numbers you need to hit so you can use them to build out this plan.

# Chapter 5

# NAVIGATE
# YOUR METRICS

Imagine two archers lined up for an archery competition. The first archer shoots ten arrows at a target. Each attempt has two likely outcomes: it either hits the target or it doesn't. The second archer shoots ten arrows aiming at nothing—just launches them into the open abyss.

Which archer won the competition? Let's break it down. Archer #1 hit the target seven times, so his accuracy was 70 percent. Archer #2 hit nothing ten times, so his accuracy was 100 percent—after all, he hit what he was aiming for, right?

Of course, there's no rational reasoning by which Archer #2 would be considered the winner. You can't judge this competition based on accuracy because that measurement is obviously irrelevant in this unique scenario. So accuracy is the wrong metric to use.

If you're working towards a specific goal, you have two likely outcomes: you'll either hit that goal or you won't. However, if you're working towards nothing, you only have one option: you'll hit nothing.

**SWAGGER TIP:** Don't shoot arrows into the abyss. Always aim for a target.

Nearly all salespeople have a set quota or goal in mind that they're working towards, so they understand how to track the exact dollar amount they still need to bring in at any given point throughout their process. At the end of the day, your quota is the bottom line, so I can't argue that it's the ultimate marker of success.

However, there are other metrics you can track to measure your progress and overall performance.

There will always be variables out of your control. I've seen brand new sales reps who were still learning the ropes but who landed large deals because something just fell into their laps. Maybe something was already in the works with a certain client, or maybe the timing was just right, so the deal was going to happen anyway. Should the sales rep in these types of situations be deemed successful? Not really.

On the flip side, sometimes deals just don't close, or take a really long time to close. I've had some deals take three years to close when the typical cycle was six to nine months. So, if you only track business that counts towards your quota, that's a great way to get frustrated.

Early on in my sales career, I imagined there had to be some way of measuring my performance even when deals weren't closing. I wanted some kind of method or formula that accounted for the various steps involved in closing a deal—because then I could look at the big picture and break it down into quarterly, monthly, weekly, and daily activities.

So I created a sales formula and started using it to track my performance. It took me several rounds of tweaking and fine-tuning before I finally got it just right, but it has been a major game-changer.

For years, the same salesman kept winning top salesperson of the year at my company's annual award event. I was still relatively new in the sales business, but I had enough things figured out to the point where I wanted to be in his shoes. I wanted to walk across the stage and receive a big trophy as the company's number one salesperson. Now, this guy was essentially a coworker of mine—even though he worked in a completely different city—so it's not like I had a vendetta against him or anything.

I simply took a picture of him on stage holding that giant trophy. I was spinning this narrative for myself that made him my worthy opponent. I compared our numbers and found out that I was already handling more accounts, closing more deals, and doing more product demos than he was. But he was still beating me because he focused on the big-ticket items, the big accounts that could potentially make the most money, and closing one or two of these accounts over the course of a year was enough to position his overall sales above mine and everyone else's.

I was winning in many different metrics but he was winning at the most important metric . . . highest percentage over quota earned. In other words, bringing in the largest amount of revenue for the company.

I'm reminded of a Brian Tracy quote that states: "A goal without a plan is only a dream." Dreaming, wishing, and wanting is great—but if you want to achieve your goals, then you need to build a plan around them. My goal was to be #1, so I started to build a plan to achieve it.

The next few sections explore the strategies I developed and explain how all of the pieces fit together. Keep in mind that the metrics and variables you should focus on might be different than the ones that I've identified, so pay more attention to the concept. And grab a notepad—because you're about to build a measurable and effective sales formula, piece by piece.

# IDENTIFY AND SIMPLIFY

I'm a big fan of John Wooden, the former UCLA basketball coach and the "put your socks on correctly" story I shared earlier. I've read and reread all of his books because his principles and life lessons are phenomenal. One that has always stuck out to me, especially in regards to sales, is to focus your efforts on the things you have 100 percent control over.

In basketball, this means not focusing on wins and losses because there are too many factors in play that determine the final score of each game, like bad referee calls or injuries. Instead, John Wooden coached his players to focus on giving their best effort every game—because that's the only metric each individual has absolute control over.

In sales, you don't have total control over the deals you close or how big or small those deals are. I can remember a major deal I had lined up with an $18 billion company that I had been doing business with for six years. I knew their buying process, and the deal was going to close in a week or two. With no prior signs or warnings, I received a call announcing that the deal was canceled because their stock hit an all-time low. They implemented a company-wide spending and hiring freeze. I was *really* counting on this deal to close and had dedicated a substantial amount of time to it, so honestly, I was devastated when I heard the news.

However, this factor was completely out of my control and had nothing to do with my performance as a salesperson. Sometimes companies just aren't in a good place financially to commit to a purchase right away. Other factors that might be stacked against you include the territory you're assigned to, the competition, or the opportunity in that area—and these factors point to more particular economic matters in the first place, such as growth and inflation. Don't get sucked into this rabbit hole of thinking and blaming about everything that is out of your control. Instead, focus on the factors you do have control over.

You need some way to track your success and achieve little wins when deals aren't closing. Because some sales cycles can last over a year, it's often difficult to gauge whether you're being effective and making the right moves. So the key is to, first, consider all of the steps you take to eventually close a deal and, second, determine which of those steps you have control over. Once you have a better sense of where you have the highest level of control, identify the one step or factor that directly correlates to deals being closed. Of course, what you identify will vary depending on your specific job and role within sales, and it might even take some reflection for you to identify this component.

For me, since I sell enterprise software, nearly every company prefers to try my software before they decide whether to purchase it or not. However, I realized that when companies do try my product, they want to buy it! In my sales process, I refer to this "try it" phase as "eval," which is short for evaluation. I'll talk more about evals later and will unpack why they're so important in closing deals. But for now, what matters is that I identified *evals* as the top, most effective component that I have control over.

So I became hyperfocused on getting more evals started and decided to track this correlation to see how it affected my overall sales. I quickly found that the more evals I performed, the more deals I closed and the more revenue I generated.

Overall, I found that nearly 50 percent of my evals turned into a closed deal within six months, so I knew that I had to get two evals started in order to close one deal, which then of course gave me the total number of evals I needed to hit. Bingo!

For five of the next six years, I hit over 200 percent of my quota. One of those years, I even received my company's #1 salesperson award—worldwide—for highest amount of revenue generated.

Even though I was hyperfocused on what I had control over, I also never lost sight of the fact that deals have to close. So when you simplify your sales process, don't get bogged down in thinking that you only have one, single action to perform. Keep other areas of your sales game sharp as well!

## QUICK-HIT ACTION

 Identify the one key metric you have
100 percent control over.

# BUILD
# YOUR FORMULA

I began to see the power in tracking my metrics, and became more diligent with them to the point where I started to build out a formula. I know this seems complex, but it actually simplified sales for me and helped me quickly focus on my business health.

I started my formula with the most important metric, what was the total amount of sales I wanted to close in the year. In my last year as a sales rep, that number was $6 million, which was 250 percent of my quota. Then I broke that number down into bite-sizable chunks—leaving me with a monthly goal of $500,000. You can break this down further by figuring out your average transaction size, and then how many transactions you need per month. My average transaction size was $250,000, so with approximately two transactions per month, my averages netted $500,000 per month.

This was significant for me to know because then I calculated that I needed four evals per month in order for two of them to convert into a closed deal.

**4 Evals/mo. → $500k/mo.**

I began to further build out my formula because there are several steps that take place before I'm able to get a prospect on board to try to evaluate my product. Logically, I started to work backward and mapped out the steps leading up to an eval starting.

Before a prospect will agree to do an eval, they obviously have to know what my product is, what it does, and what value it has within their company—duh! All of this takes place during my demo presentation, which is the step right before the eval phase.

It was rather straightforward that, in order to get an eval, I needed to do more demos. So I began to track my demos to determine how many demos it took to land an eval. I realized that one of every two demos turned into an eval within six months, so my formula expanded to:

**2 Demos/wk. → 4 Evals/mo. → $500k/mo.**

Then I wanted to map this back to prospecting because demos don't just happen on their own. I had to prospect and regularly reach out to prospects to get sales conversations, or discovery calls. Successful discovery calls led to demos. I wanted to keep my formula as simple as possible without tracking too many things.

I started tracking my prospecting, how many I reached out to and how many connections I got. It caused me to really fine-tune this process so that for every five new prospects I reached out to, I'd eventually get two demos from those efforts. That's an exceptionally high percentage to achieve in my company, but I only came upon it by tracking it.

So my formula expanded once again and became:

| 5 Prospects/wk. → 2 Demos/wk. → 4 Evals/mo. → $500k/mo. |
| --- |

This is my complete formula. I told you it was simple! But don't overlook the amount of information that is actually contained in this formula. This formula tells me how many prospects I need to reach out to each week, how many demos I should be performing each week, how many evals should be started each month, and how much in revenue I should be closing each month.

Just a quick reminder that your activity metrics might be different, but the formula you build should still operate the same way once you identify the activities that lead to closing deals in your specific line of work—the activities that help you achieve the amount of business you're aiming for. And keep it simple! You don't want a long, drawn out formula that is difficult to track and measure. A formula that looks like a quadratic equation won't excite anyone to sell!

The whole reason to measure and track these activities is to see what areas you're weak in and make adjustments. This is your own data to help optimize every component of your selling game.

It took me a long time to devise this sales formula from scratch and build it out the first time. Trust me, I didn't just figure it out overnight. Initially, the only factor I started with was my quota and how much I still needed to sell that year. I worked backwards from that point and formed estimations for the other components just to get things started. Then I just kept fine-tuning the formula by tweaking the numbers based on the data.

Eventually, my sales formula caused other realizations to surface. For example, I realized that I needed to finetune my demos in order to get buy-in from my prospects. And because I was constantly fine-tuning and tweaking things in this formula the whole time, it made me up my game—one area at a time.

You want to see the activity metrics so you're working to move the needle every day.

What you don't measure, you can't improve.

I learned this principle from reading Peter Drucker's work (if you don't know him, look him up!). However, when it comes to sales, it's important to note that the items I tracked in the formula were two sides of a coin—they either happened or they didn't.

For instance, it's difficult to accurately measure your pipeline of new opportunities because there's too much human intervention involved when it comes down to those metrics. You want to keep your formula simple and in a "yes or no" metric, so don't track too many things.

I had my business consistently humming. It was a machine that couldn't be stopped . . . and it was also fun! When you get to this point, you truly achieve swagger. I was consistently performing demos, getting evals started, and closing two or three deals a month. My swagger was serious!

Once you do all the initial work to set up your sales formula, measure and track, measure and track, measure and track. It's that simple.

## QUICK-HIT ACTION

 Build your formula—then measure
and track your activity.

## TOP 10 LIST

As I've said, I'm kind of cerebral when it comes to data and statistics. Tracking all of my numbers to measure certain areas of my sales game has helped me tremendously, but I'm always reminding myself that the "best" metrics don't necessarily equate to a specific dollar amount. For example, when I examined the top-earning salespeople in my company, I found that most of them closed one major deal that accounted for more than half of their entire annual quota.

My colleagues and I call this "whale hunting."

You have to know where the potential for big deals are—because one big deal feeds the entire tribe.

So, after a few years of sticking to my sales formula and constantly refining it, I had enough data to see patterns, read between the numbers, and narrow down where the best potential was for big deals. This sparked my first *Top 10 Opportunity* list of big deals, which I continue to create each year.

I largely focus my efforts around this list. Each week, I review my potential big deals and take actions specifically catered to those accounts and prospects.

The big deals that I'm talking about don't just happen spontaneously.

Compared to other prospects and customers, those on your Top 10 list will require significantly more attention and effort before they're ready to make a major purchase.

And, if I'm doing something every week that moves them closer to the next big deal, some will happen over time. Big deals take time, that's just how it is. That is why it is so important to do at least one thing every week.

I figured with a list of ten large deals, I wasn't going to close them all. It's just not very realistic. Further, some might take two or three years to close. However, if I'm able to close three out of ten deals or even just two out of ten deals, then I'll for sure crush my quota! So this list became central to my sales mindset.

The Top 10 list are usually big companies where lots of people and decision-makers will be involved. It might even require an executive group of twenty or thirty people in a company aligning in a decision to move forward with a purchase. It takes time to get to know those people, identify their needs, and build trust.

As the salesperson, be active in this process and keep taking initiatives to move the needle forward. It's important to pop up on their radar frequently, so check in with different individuals each week, and make yourself available to meet with key members, as needed.

Although landing just two or three deals from your Top 10 list is big money, be mindful to not put all of your eggs in one basket. If you *only* focus on the accounts listed on your Top 10 list, and you're counting on three big deals to follow through, it will be quite the sucker punch if one of those deals doesn't convert.

Your *whale hunting* expedition might take months to complete, so keep your fishing hook in shallower waters so that you and your family can stay fed.

Your other, smaller accounts help the dollars trickle in throughout the year, while you're working towards deals on your Top 10. I tend to reach the majority of my quota each year with one or two big deals from my Top 10 list, but I still manage between thirty or forty accounts total in order to keep my pipeline flowing.

Each week, spend your focused time and effort on your Top 10 opportunities, and then work all of your other accounts and prospects into a rotation, depending on each one's individual needs. Touching base with each one at least once every few weeks. For the bottom 10 percent, once a quarter is usually sufficient, but determine the frequency you need for each one.

Lastly, look for ways to bulk-action smaller accounts together. For example, you don't want to spend a lot of time planning a sales event around one of the smaller accounts, because it probably won't reap the benefits necessary to match your effort. But you could invite several smaller accounts to a sales event you structured around one of your Top 10 clients. I've had positive results in this exact scenario, so think outside the box and use the resources and capabilities you have at your disposal.

## QUICK-HIT ACTION

 Build a Top 10 Opportunity List—
and go whale hunting!

Now that you understand how to start building your strategic sales formula, let's get after it by taking your prospecting to the next level.

# Chapter 6

# ENHANCE YOUR PROSPECTING

I was fortunate in that I knew the importance of optimizing my work routine even before I began my sales career. I learned a lot from Tim Ferris's *The 4-Hour Workweek*, which dives deep into the "how" side of optimizing your workweek. Before Tim Ferris wrote this book, he had a job in sales and realized there were numerous ways for salespeople to optimize their work routine. The whole premise of his book is taking a forty-hour workweek and compressing it down into a four-hour workweek while still achieving the same results.

When Tim performed prospecting calls, he only reached out during "peak times" when people were most likely to answer the phone. Figuring out these times took attentiveness and trial and error, but he was eventually able to read between the lines to understand the general trends. For instance, between 7 a.m. and 8 a.m., people often answered the phone because they were sipping coffee at their desk and hadn't fully emerged into their workday yet. Another successful time frame was during lunch, because people already had their phone out checking voice or text messages. So he only called during these times, while his colleagues were making phone calls all day.

Once he figured out these metrics, he ended up making fewer calls over a shorter period of time than his peers, and he got better results.

The point is to read between the lines in order to work smarter. Here's a third example to really drive this point home for today's workforce: there are some executives who are in back-to-back meetings all day so connecting with them during the workday is nearly impossible. But you might be able to catch them after 5 p.m. or when they might be driving home from work. I've even found a trend with some executives being active on their email on Sunday mornings or evenings in order to catch up on email or jumpstart the workweek. Sending an email around then was a viable option because I knew they would naturally see it.

**SWAGGER TIP:** Be strategic with your prospecting to improve your connection rate.

Prospecting builds your pipeline of incoming clients and sales, so it's one of the most important factors in the entire sales process. I've never seen a down-in-the-dumps salesperson who has a full pipeline of opportunities.

However, prospecting is one of those tasks that most salespeople intend to do but struggle to actually get done. It can be difficult to gauge how urgent prospecting is compared to other pressing tasks because—unlike your boss, coworkers, and other customers—prospects aren't contacting you throughout the day or waiting on you to fulfill a request.

It's too easy to get caught up with all the other tasks that seem "pressing" while continuing to push back your prospecting time to another day or week. This is one of the biggest mistakes you can make as a salesperson, because rather than reaching out to prospects, you're handling tedious tasks. Believe me, there will always be tedious tasks to take care of, but they can wait.

Prospecting equals new opportunities, and these new opportunities directly impact your quota. So if you want to crush your quota, don't let other tasks take over your prospecting time slots. Schedule the time to do it and stick to it!

Start with blocking out the time. This matter is simple, but get it on your task list and add it to your agenda each week before other tasks. The next step is even simpler—just do it! If you find yourself putting it off or skipping it occasionally, I recommend handling it first thing in the morning. Get it out of the way so you're not tempted to procrastinate about it later in the day.

I've been guilty of telling myself, "Tomorrow I'm going to do my prospecting," but when tomorrow comes, I get busy with email, a few customer requests, and then maybe my boss calls and tells me to update the CRM. Long story short, by 4 p.m., I'm tired, and the workday is coming to a close. So, once again, I tell myself, "I'll just do my prospecting tomorrow."

Are you seeing the cycle? I think we've all been there. The bottom line is that you have to schedule it *and* have the discipline to stick to it.

I've seen too many sales reps scramble at the end of a quarter to close deals. I'm not saying to make prospecting a higher priority than closing deals, or anything else for that matter, but if you don't prospect for a few weeks you will feel the results later. You won't see the negative impact now, but weeks or months from now you'll feel it when you don't have deals closing because of a weak pipeline.

Prospecting was a key to developing my swagger. I got to the point where I believed I could get a meeting with anyone. They might not want to meet when I want, and it will take some time, but eventually my value proposition will be strong enough to get that meeting. You can get a meeting with anyone. Maybe not immediately or the first time you reach out to someone, but given enough time, all of the actions you've performed will work in your favor.

There was one account that I spent three years prospecting twenty to thirty different people before I finally got my foot in the door and closed the deal. Now that's a long sales cycle! But that one deal was $3.17 million, which was 160 percent of my quota that year. So was all that hard work and rejection worth it?

Absolutely, yes!

I remember another company where I spent about a year and a half calling and emailing different people before I finally made initial contact with someone who answered the phone. I was actually caught off guard when I heard a voice on the other end—because, again, I had been reaching out for a year and a half with no response, ever.

Not long into this call, I had piqued the prospect's interest enough to schedule a demo presentation. When I arrived on-site to do the demo, he greeted me at the front lobby before the two of us walked through the main office stacked with cubicles. As we were doing so, I took notice of each of the name tags on the cubicles, and I had a peculiar sensation of seeing several names I recognized.

I realized, *Oh! I reached out to her a year ago—but she never responded. I reached out to this guy, too—no response. And, yep, those are two more names I remember emailing.* And when I started the demo a few minutes later, all of these individuals were present in the conference room.

No one seemed to make the connection that I had tried to contact them earlier—but if they did, they did a good job of masking it. At the end of the demo, I heard two or three of the coworkers comment to one another, saying things like, "Wow, what a great product," and "I wish we would have had this software a year or two ago!"

I was amused and had to refrain from saying, "Well, you could have had this product last year! If only you would have answered my emails and calls eighteen months ago." It was very satisfying to close a large transaction a few months later with this account after all that persistence.

That is the job of prospecting, or as some call it "the hunt." When you finally make that connection and get the meeting, it feels amazing!

There are many books dedicated to just prospecting. Some of my favorite authors include Jeb Blount, Mark Hunter, Chet Holmes, Anthony Iannarino, and Mike Weinberg. I won't get into the level of depth and detail that they do, but

I certainly wanted to cover some key prospecting tips in this chapter.

Keep in mind that prospecting is a critical piece of your sales formula. The following sections will help you be more effective in your reach outs in order to achieve the most demo meetings (or next whatever the next step is in your sales process):

---

**5 Prospects/wk. ➜ 2 Demos/wk.**

---

## GIVE TO GET

Many salespeople fail at prospecting because they are too focused on what they want—a meeting with a potential client. In other words, looking even further down the stretch, what they actually want is to land a sale. This approach often causes potential clients to run the other way. We've all been approached by the "pushy" salesperson who spends more time praising their product or service rather than discovering your needs and if what they're selling can benefit you.

Think about this quote from Zig Ziglar, "You can have everything you want in life, if you will just help enough other people get what they want."

When you genuinely focus on helping and providing value to others, they'll naturally be inclined to do business with you. The more you give to others, the more you will get what you want in return—it's a direct correlation!

So how do you do this?

I do my best to provide value to prospects at every interaction. I actively seek out what's causing them stress and struggle in order to understand their goals, needs, and objectives. Then I tell them how I've helped others solve those issues.

I've personally experienced a much higher response rate when I've done this. When you request a meeting, you're *asking* someone for their time, energy, and engagement. However, if you *offer* to solve someone's problem or help them achieve a goal, they'll be more likely to give you some of their time. So if a prospect is not responding, assume that you haven't showcased enough value yet.

Inviting someone to a sales event or workshop is a great way to communicate that you are offering them something valuable, rather than *asking* for something. You're simply trying to achieve that first step, or at least the next step, with a new prospect, but the receptiveness and response you receive from prospects, will largely depend on the approach you choose.

People love to get out of the office for a few hours to go to a business-related event, so I often work events into my prospecting cadence. I've hosted panel discussion events for prospects and customers to gather and share their expertise and best practices. I've taught workshop events at universities, where individuals could learn a new technical skill and get a certification. I've even put together networking opportunities to help like-minded business professionals connect with one another.

All of those events offered a value-added component to them, and that positions me as more of a consultant than a salesperson.

## QUICK-HIT ACTION

 Offer value to achieve higher
response rates.

## RESEARCH + REACH OUT

There are two components you should primarily think about when you sit down to prospect new contacts each week: research and reach out.

Research is obviously the baseline objective you need to handle to discover new leads, contact info, and other important details, but don't spend your entire prospecting session just gathering information. I've heard too many salespeople proudly proclaim that they spent two or three hours prospecting—but then when I ask them a few questions about how it went, I quickly learn that they spent two or three hours on research.

If you don't reach out to anyone, this isn't prospecting! Pair your research with the actual outbound action of reaching out.

Reaching out is measurable, trackable, and goal-oriented.

At a minimum, I do a ninety-minute and a sixty-minute prospecting session each week. My measurable goal is to send an email out every thirty minutes because I want to ensure that I'm reaching out to at least five new prospects every week. That disciplines me to be quick with the research side of the task so I can stay on target by sending something out.

Use email templates and tailor existing emails that worked to help you achieve this pace. Hold yourself to the thirty-minute rule, and don't spend too much time writing up the perfect email because most people won't reply to it. You do want to be diligent and have it be very targeted to the prospect, but this can be accomplished in thirty minutes. It often takes twelve to fifteen reach outs before a prospect finally responds, so don't waste time trying to make your initial email perfect.

If possible, use intros that mention referrals rather than reaching out "cold"; these will always have higher response rates. When you don't have referrals, use Google, LinkedIn, and other online tools to do your research and cater your email. You want your message to be uniquely targeted to the prospect, their company, and their role within that company. If the message is too general, the prospect might assume that you've sent out an email blast to a number of contacts on an email list, and then they'll be less likely to respond.

However, there is no silver bullet, nor is there one magical phrase that gets you a meeting every time. I literally had an email that worked for one prospect, and then I sent it to someone else with the same role at a similar company and received no response. So don't analyze your emails too critically. Some prospects will respond, some won't—so what! Move on.

My emails are pretty basic. I try to identify a possible need or potential goal and then note how I can be of service in that situation. I point out my credibility in that area and how I've helped others with a similar need or goal. The result I'm looking for is to get the prospect interested in talking with me.

To provide an example, here's a copy of an actual email that I sent to the VP of an $8 billion insurance company. Recognize how quickly I established a connection and got to the point on why we should meet. It's short, concise, and takes minimal time away from someone's day.

> Subject: Mark <lastname> from <company1>
>
> Hi Tom,
>
> I came across your LinkedIn profile because we share a connection with a friend, Mark <lastname>. You must know him from when you worked at <company1>?
>
> I noticed your infrastructure role at <company2> and background with ITSM. Our integration with ServiceNow has helped <customer1> reduce their <problem>. We are able to <benefit explanation>.
>
> Locally, I work with <customer2>, <customer3>, and <customer4>. What's the best way to set up a time to discuss?
>
> -Tim
> <phone number>

I often end my emails by asking for a nine-minute phone call. I request a phone call because more prospects will agree to that rather than an in-person meeting. And why nine minutes and not ten? Because ten minutes is generic—nine minutes is unique and stands out! I figure most people are willing to give less than ten minutes for something that can benefit them.

But I imagine the one thing you really want to know in this section is . . . did that VP of the $8 billion company respond back to my email?

Oh, he responded back alright. This email landed me a meeting with him that eventually led to a huge sale!

## QUICK-HIT ACTION

Hold yourself accountable to sending a targeted email every thirty minutes.

## TRACK & FOLLOW UP

Research shows that it can often take twelve to fifteen reach outs before a prospect finally responds.

As the salesperson, you want to show the prospect some urgency but without being annoying or a pest. This is a fine line, but it's critical because no one wants to talk to a pushy, overbearing salesperson. That being said, the key to connecting with a prospect is being persistent and creative with your follow-ups.

Utilize a CRM or spreadsheet for tracking your follow-up cadence. Each week, I spend thirty to sixty minutes solely dedicated to following up with prospects. Here is the nine-week cadence I use that leads to a connection with two out of every five prospects:

| Week 1 | Email #1 |
|--------|----------|
| Week 2 | Email #2 + Voicemail #1 |
| Week 3 | LinkedIn message #1 + Voicemail #2 |
| Week 4 | Email #3 + Direct mail #1 |
| Week 5 | Email #4 + LinkedIn message #2 |
| Week 6 | Email #5 + Voicemail #3 |
| Week 7 | Direct mail #2 |
| Week 8 | Email #6 + LinkedIn message #3 |
| Week 9 | Email #7 + Voicemail #4 |

My follow-up emails weren't just, "Did you get my email?" I often try to add more value points on why they should talk to me based on additional research I did. Follow-up emails and messaging take five minutes or less, which is much quicker than the initial thirty-minute email. Again, you want your messaging to be very clear, calculated, and to the point about why the prospect should talk with you. Always add value, and make your messaging very unique and different. Show them you've done your research and you are a credible resource that can help them.

Voicemails were also a critical mechanism in helping me build credibility to get connections. I didn't expect people to call me back, but I wanted them to hear that I wasn't a cheesy, pushy salesperson. I follow Jill Konrath's tips about keeping voicemails under thirty seconds.

LinkedIn is another one of my key mechanisms for prospecting. If I haven't heard back from a prospect after two reach outs, I'll send a LinkedIn message as the third reach out. Because you can be a little less formal with LinkedIn messaging vs. email, here's an example of what I might say: "I'm messaging you here because maybe your company spam filter is blocking me? I practice responsible email habits...I promise!"

Notice the touch of humor in that message? Let me just say that humor often works when nothing else will. Humor is a great way to stand out and grab someone's attention with your reach out. There have been several instances where I've used a humorous reach out approach and then finally received a response back from a prospect.

One of my all-time favorite approaches is mailing a prospect a small trash can. They open this box they've received in the mail, find a trash can, and are beyond confused until they see the crumpled-up piece of paper—rather, piece of trash—in the trash can. When they grab that single piece of trash out of the trash can and smooth out the paper, they find a note that reads: "Hi _____, I figured you'd throw my letter away, so I thought I'd save you the trouble."

Of course, the note then has a few more sentences with my contact information and brief pitch, but put yourself in the shoes of the prospect receiving this trash can and note in the mail! I've done this several times and have received multiple responses. I mean, wouldn't you respond to something like this?

In addition to humor, here are some other creative reach out ideas that will help you stand out.

A handwritten note sent through the mail can be a true game-changer because most salespeople don't think of it or won't take the extra two minutes to stamp and mail the envelope—because email just makes everything too easy! Another idea is to look up a prospect's alma mater and send them a coffee mug with a brief and witty note attached. It's a small gift that might lead to a big sale down the road. I've heard of sales reps sending a shoe with a handwritten note saying, "Just trying to get my foot in the door."

By week nine, I send a "farewell" email and then stop reaching out, and you'd be surprised how many people ignore all of my previous contact attempts but respond back to this one. My email and voicemail say something like, "You are either too busy or not interested, so this is my last reach out. If you truly are interested, let me know and we can set up a future time to chat."

If you run through this cadence with a prospect and they don't respond, you probably don't want to talk with them anyway ... they are dull! Maybe not? Well, then you can always reach out to them again in a couple of months with new reasons and messaging tactics.

Have an abundance mentality, move on, and reach out to someone else.

## QUICK-HIT ACTION

Be persistent and creative with
your follow-ups.

That's a wrap on Part II: Define Your Grind. In Part III, we dive into aligning everything together so you can operate swiftly in moving prospects through your sales process and towards closed deals. We start by detailing the discovery call.

# Part III

# ALIGN YOUR DESIGN

# Chapter 7

# MASTER YOUR DISCOVERY CALL

In tennis, if the ball is on your side of the court, you're losing. You want to keep sending the ball over to your opponent's side of the court and strategically place it so your opponent has to decide how to maneuver. If you do this persistently, your opponent will eventually make an error or hit a weak shot that you can easily put away to win the point.

Discovery calls are similar. It's oftentimes your first live conversation with a prospect who has succumbed to your persistent outreach. You want to be very strategic with the time you have their attention and guide the conversation with questions that will keep the ball on their side of the court . . . so you can get the big win.

What I mean is this: if you're doing all of the talking, your prospect defaults to an "audience mindset," which means they're just waiting for the show to end so they can exit the theater and get back to something more important. You don't want your prospect to be in "waiting" mode—because waiting mode quickly transitions to "not even listening" mode.

Instead, you want to flip this dynamic by engaging your prospect in a productive conversation. Hit the tennis ball to their side of the court. You want them to talk, yes, but you want to draw them out in a certain way. A sales call where you're talking ninety percent of the time is not going to get you anywhere. You need to identify your potential client's needs and solve their problem. The most effective way to do this is to get them talking about the issues and problems they currently deal with and then showcasing how your product can solve their concerns.

**SWAGGER TIP:** Ask strategic questions to keep the ball on your opponent's court to get the big win.

Discovery calls and prospecting go hand in hand to get you the right amount of demos. The ultimate goal is to have a follow-up call or better yet, book a demo. If you don't come prepared, it's likely you won't achieve either of these objectives and might not get an opportunity with this prospect for a very long time.

Usually, a discovery call shouldn't last more than twenty minutes, but I might spend an hour or two preparing for it to make sure I have my every move nailed down. I've mastered my discovery calls to where I'm always able to book the next steps, but this wasn't always the case.

The discovery call is a pretty significant milestone in the selling process. It incorporates several concepts that you've learned earlier in this book and puts them into action. So let's walk through an outline of the perfect discovery call.

Let me first note that I refer to it as a discovery "call" because, in my case, nearly all of these meetings occur over a phone call. However, there are plenty of salespeople across different fields who regularly have this same type of meeting with prospects in person, often over coffee or lunch.

It's also important to recognize that most discovery calls begin with the prospect not being interested in what you're selling. So your mindset around this call should be to take them from "not interested" to realizing they "need it desperately."

If you followed my advice in Chapter 6, you set up a nine-minute discovery call. This may sound a bit over the top, but set a timer for nine minutes! And then, at the nine-minute mark exactly, stop in mid-sentence to state that the nine minutes is up, and then ask them if they need to hop off the phone or if they have a few more minutes to wrap up the discussion. The customer will appreciate your consideration of their time and will almost always spare a few more minutes for you to finish the call. Most of my discovery calls end up going fifteen to twenty minutes.

Right before your call is about to begin, remember that your initial objective should be to *make a friend*. So start the call off casually and with friendly conversation. Introduce yourself, try to make a connection, and continue on.

Look for a natural opening in the conversation to transition away from the chit-chat and into delivering your values statement (I go over everything you need to know about crafting a values statement in a section below). I've found that a gentle way to make this transition while still keeping a casual tone is to "explain" where you're steering the question but in an "asking" manner. Here's an example of what I mean: "Well, how about I give you a thirty-second intro about my product/service and how it helps customers similar to you? I'll then ask you a couple questions to see if there's a fit, and also answer any of your questions. How does that sound?"

Assuming they say yes (they always do!), you would then deliver your values statement, which, in short, is a quick pitch that overviews your product/service. I'll get into the values statement shortly, but for now, the key is to be quick.

Even though you've only talked for a moment up to this point, turn the conversation back over to them and *find a need*. Avoid asking yes or no questions. Ask "how" questions, because these are the types of questions that keep them talking. This keeps the ball on their side of the court, which keeps the conversation interesting for them. Remember, "how" questions bring the pain points to the surface, so prepare these questions intentionally.

Try to answer or respond to one of their pains/problems with a customer story. If they're hesitant to tell you about their pains and problems, say something like, "Wow, I'm impressed at how smooth your operation is compared to most of my other clients." This kind of statement always jolts their attention and even disarms them, because they don't know exactly how to reply to it.

This scenario is now the perfect opportunity to insert a customer story. Position it as a similar client or company and describe how your product/service fits into their ecosystem to solve problems.

Most likely, the prospect you're talking to will casually agree that they have the same problem you just described in the story, or they'll at least bring up a similar problem that you can work with and talk more about. Answer with another story, if you can, but overall, make sure to portray how you can help them solve something within their business.

Tell them you'd like to build a custom demo to showcase your product/service in action and how it might be the solution they need to optimize their business.

The last step is critical: book a follow-up meeting before ending the call. If the call ends and there's no follow-up meeting on the calendar, it's very likely it will never happen. Even if they say, "We'll get back to you," they probably won't. The best-case scenario is usually that you'll follow up three or four times to get a response. Remember this acronym: BAMFAM. I dive into this concept in one of the sections below, but in short, BAMFAM will teach you how to casually insist on booking a follow-up meeting without sounding too pushy.

Don't try to wing a discovery call without planning, because they're way too important. Every discovery call I have leads to some type of opportunity because I come so well prepared. So use these notes like an outline and practice navigating the meeting's conversation! Grab a colleague and rehearse a few mock discovery calls.

Now let's get into some key components of the discovery call to make sure you book the next step.

# BE
# PREPARED!

You've spent all this time prospecting, you finally have a meeting lined up with someone important, and then you hop on the call and "wing it"?

I've seen far too many salespeople do this over and over again and it drives me crazy! That's why there's an exclamation point attached to the title of this section—so you can imagine me yelling, "Be prepared!"

How can you do all that work and then not take the time to prepare for the moment where you can finally get the outcome you've been working towards? As a salesperson, you usually don't have the odds in your favor, so you have to be strategic in your approach. If you make a bad impression or don't establish some value, it might be two years before you get another opportunity to converse with this specific prospect. Trust me, it's happened to me before.

I fully expect that every intro call or meeting I have will end with the prospect being interested in my product. In my mind, this outcome occurs every time because that's just how I think. I truly believe it's the only likely scenario to happen—so that's why it happens.

Of course, there are times when this first call doesn't play out exactly like I'd like it to, but I quickly forget those calls and keep moving forward! You get what you expect, so expect that they'll be interested. If my strategy was to "wing it" or "hope for the best," my results would be different.

Do all of your research and preparation upfront.

Look into their company to pinpoint potential needs. Examine the role of the person you'll be speaking with to try to discern what their specific needs might be. Identify business goals and objectives that your product or service can help with.

Many prospects will have objections and might be hesitant to meet with you again. Don't be caught off guard when this happens. With the right preparation, you can handle some objections before the prospect even brings them up. If you're like me, you'll hear the same objections from different prospects all the time, so I've come up with responses that keep the prospect engaged and interested.

If there isn't urgency to meet again, find a way to stay in touch. I'll often tell them about my networking group and invite them to the next meeting so they can meet Person A or Individual B. This tactic keeps the conversation open and has a strong possibility for a meeting in the future.

Prepare! Prepare! Prepare!

## VALUE STATEMENT

"So let me ask you this—what keeps you up at night?"

Has anyone ever asked you this before? Has a *salesperson* ever asked you this before?

This question has actually become a punchline among me and some of my coworkers because it's one of the biggest pitfalls-of-a-question that a salesperson can ask. It shows your lack of preparation and truly understanding your prospect. Don't be the cheesy salesperson who asks this question—and don't be the cheesy salesperson who believes that this question is a great hook to kick off a discovery meeting with a new prospect.

Develop a refined value statement that quickly portrays what your product does. Your value statement should be short but very sharp like an "elevator pitch," so that it hooks prospects and intrigues them enough to want to hear more.

It may take a few rewrites to get it sounding just right, but once it's refined, practice it! Rehearse it over and over again for days until you have it memorized. And then keep rehearsing it. The goal is to have it memorized so well that you can pitch it with confidence every time.

Even when you have it memorized, record yourself to hear how it sounds. Listen to see if your tone and delivery is as smooth as possible and enunciated clearly. If all of these details sound excessive, it's because your value statement is that important.

Remember this saying: "The song you play is more important than the words you say." This speaks to the overall poise, confidence, and swagger of your delivery. What interrupts your song is "ums" and "ahs" because they come across as unsure or nervous. However, what makes your song resonate is having an overall good vibe and well-balanced personal energy. Pay attention to these matters, but don't go too far with being overly enthusiastic.

Also, don't use business jargon or acronyms. You want your value statement to be simple and easy to understand for the audience. I like to say that it needs to be simple enough for my third-grade daughter to understand it. Your delivery of it should make you stand out as a non-cheesy salesperson. You will come across as a knowledgeable consultant who can likely help them.

I've found that many salespeople want to rant on and on to go over everything about their product. Don't do this up front! It's too much and too confusing. Pick the top two highlights that your product does and showcase those in your value statement. Anything more than two points won't likely be remembered.

Overall—be focused on the value your solution provides.

## QUICK-HIT ACTION

Record, rehearse, and memorize
your value statement.

## BAMFAM

Book A Meeting From A Meeting—BAMFAM!

I've seen too many salespeople get frustrated because a prospect won't reply to their request for a meeting. Clients are crazy busy and usually have a lot of priorities already stacked up. If you've had a successful discovery call and established a need that you can solve, why didn't you book another meeting on the spot?

The purpose of BAMFAM is to schedule a follow-up meeting as you wrap up your conversation with a potential client. If you don't take BAMFAM seriously, there may not ever be another meeting—because you'll be out the door and then quickly out of their mind!

A great way to get discouraged is by going back and forth with a client over a string of emails just trying to find a mutual time to schedule a meeting. This scenario takes up way too much time because you didn't BAMFAM.

We've all been in the "email me some times that work for you" situation, right? So you email your availability, days go by, most of your time slots have been filled in the meantime, and then you receive an email back about meeting soon—but the time slot they selected is now filled. And the cycle continues. Without a doubt, this is a very inefficient use of your time, especially if you're constantly in this ongoing cycle with several prospects.

Additionally, this situation changes your posture and makes you look like the "needy" salesperson chasing prospects down to set up a meeting. This is not the posture you want, trust me! Remember that you're offering value, your time is valuable, and you're not charging anyone any money just for meetings—so you don't want to portray yourself in "chase-mode." When you BAMFAM, you easily avoid this whole dynamic.

Instead, as you wrap up a discovery call or a similar type of meeting, say something like, "Let me pull up my calendar" or, "Do you have your calendar handy?" And suggest a span of days that might be good to have a follow-up meeting.

How the prospect responds will help you gauge their level of interest, so you know how to respond next.

You don't want to be too pushy if the client is sounding hesitant. Suggest a tentative meeting a few weeks down the road. If the client says, "Let me get back to you in six months," it's a pretty clear indication that they're not very interested in what you have to offer. However, ask if you can set a placeholder meeting date on the calendar six months from now. Be considerate with how you approach this request. It might even be best to make a joke about yourself like, "My memory isn't as good as it used to be, so if I don't get it on my calendar, I'm sure I'll forget."

Getting a meeting on the books and then having to reschedule it later is no big deal. At the very least, it gives you another excuse to reach out to them down the road.

I prefer a super casual approach about the whole matter and most often say something like, "Let's make it easy and meet at this same time one week from today." The simple logic I default to here is that, since this block was open in their calendar this week, it's likely to also be available next week.

Be proactive about setting those next steps, but don't keep chasing someone in circles about the next meeting.

Act like your time is valuable—because your time is valuable—and your clients will pick up on that vibe and meet you halfway. This will for sure increase your swagger!

## QUICK-HIT ACTION

**Book yourself solid with
BAMFAM!**

If you follow what you've learned in this chapter, you'll make all the right moves to intrigue your prospect about learning more and seeing more. You've got to nail the next steps in order to successfully showcase your product or service.

# Chapter 8

# NAIL YOUR DEMO

We live in a *see it—try it—buy it!* type of society. Whether they know it or not, most individuals need to go through this process anytime they're debating making a large purchase.

Think about buying a car: maybe you've seen ads for a new model of car you've never driven before, and now you're hooked on it! How likely are you to call a dealership and just purchase that car on the spot? Not likely, I assume, because you've never seen it up close and you've never driven it. However, if you visit the dealership, test drive the car, and are still hooked on it, you're much more likely to buy it. You feel more comfortable spending your money after you've tried the product you're buying.

Plus, people buy things emotionally, not intellectually. So getting people to "try it" engages those emotions.

Seeing that shiny new car in person, sitting in it, and smelling that "new car" smell stirs your emotions. Then you test drive it and fall in love with it, and boom—your emotions are peaked and you want it!

I've mentioned that most of my sales experience has been centered around selling enterprise software. Most executives and decision makers at the companies I reach out to don't spend a lot of time browsing the web for new software, so the demo meeting is often a significant game-changer for me. It's my opportunity to showcase the "see it" phase and then immediately lead them into the "try it" phase.

**SWAGGER TIP:** Lean into the *see it—try it—buy it!* mindset and see how your sales increase.

Remember the sales formula. You want to have effective demos because they lead to more evals. This chapter outlines some key concepts so you can get an eval started for every other demo:

> ### 2 Demos/wk. ➜ 1 Eval/wk.

Before I fine-tuned my demo process, persuading new prospects to move forward with next steps was challenging. All of my demos seemed to end the same way—the client thanked me for the presentation, said that they'll need some time to meet with their team and think things over, and then, nearly verbatim, said, "So we'll get back to you sometime next week." And of course, as you've probably already guessed, they usually didn't follow up with me "next week" or even within a few weeks. Not even when I reached back out to them.

Sometimes I had to drive two hours across the region to do these demos, and then had to leave completely empty handed. No solid next steps, plans, or action items were agreed on. Those long drives back home are brutal when you don't have any kind of win or nugget of success to account for.

But I was conducting those meetings completely wrong. I finally took a step back and dissected my demo meetings to try to understand the dynamics of what wasn't working. In those early days, I was just following the basic guide rails that my company set up or was relying too much on my sales engineer to run the meeting.

My demo meetings lasted sixty to ninety minutes. I took a sales engineer with me to dive into some of the specifics, and I never really had an end-of-meeting plan once the pitch was done. As it turns out, this is exactly the type of meeting you DON'T want to have when it comes to the demo.

The last thing you want to be is the visiting salesperson putting on a "dog and pony show." At this phase, you're still trying to reel in the customer with bite-size pieces, so an hour or more is way too long and extravagant.

Realize that most people will have an attention span of seven to ten minutes before they zone out, check their phone, and check you off their list. However, also realize that most of the office personnel you visit consider their workday boring, so you have the chance to liven it up a bit by being memorable without being obnoxious.

The first time I went to a demo meeting without my sales engineer, I finally had a breakthrough in understanding the demo process and the surrounding circumstances. I prepared for this meeting by taking screenshots on an iPad to quickly showcase my company's software in action. Because I did my homework (that's a subtle reminder to all of you salespeople), the screenshots pinpointed how my product could solve this organization's pains and problems.

This particular meeting was just a one-on-one situation with me and the VP of the company. The demo I put together only consisted of using the iPad while talking through each of the screenshots. It lasted fifteen minutes and I had the customer engaged like no one I had pitched to before with my sales engineer present. I mean, this client was *hooked!*

He was so excited that he asked me if I could wait a few minutes while he grabbed the company's lead architect. He darted down the office hallway, had a few words with this guy, then came back and said, "He can't join us right now, but when can you meet next?"

I had a follow-up meeting where the VP had several other decision makers present, and it wasn't long before we completed the eval and sealed the deal. And the best part of closing this deal was that there was no dog and pony show in the process!

From then on, I decided to do my own demos more often. I continue this trend today because it further sends a message to the prospect that my product is easy and simple to use. In fact, I often say, "If the dumb sales guy can demo this product, it must be easy!"

Customize a short demo instead of a one-size-fits-all lengthy demo. Your demo should magnify specific pains, needs, and goals of your client. You want them to see and believe how your product can help them. As far as content goes—less is more. If it takes you sixty minutes to show how your product can help them, it makes your product seem complex. This probably isn't going to be appealing to them because their work-life is already busy and complex. If you can display the value and high points of your product/service in a quick, ten-minute demo, it will come across as clear, simple, and exciting—which is how you want your client to *feel* about your product/service during and immediately after your presentation.

You don't want to perform a demo and then have nothing transpire because of it. Your goal is to get to the next meeting, what I call the eval planning meeting. Have an end-of-demo plan that continues to guide the customer all the way through and into the next steps.

The three following sections are the keys to ensuring you nail the demo and get your prospect to proceed with the eval phase.

## SET
## EXPECTATIONS

Understand the dynamics of a demo meeting compared to, let's say, a discovery call or even a follow-up discovery meeting. Most often, the discovery phase involves you and one other point of contact. The demo phase, however, usually involves a group of people within that company whom you haven't met before. Maybe they had the option and chose to sit in on your demo presentation or maybe it was mandatory, but in either case, each person in the audience is always wondering what's going to happen. That being said, it's critical to start the meeting out "the right way" while you have everyone's attention.

In other words, there is a strategic way that will help you achieve the desired results of the meeting, and it largely has to do with your opening statements and how you use them to segway into the rest of your demo.

Most attendees will quickly realize that you're a salesperson because of how you're dressed and the fact that you're presenting. They probably don't know you, and the last sales guy talked too much, so they might naturally tune you out quickly. More common than not, here are some of the areas where their minds might wonder towards:

*What exactly is this meeting about anyway?*

*I'm busy—how much time is this presentation going to take? Is it going to be worth my attention?*

*What's my excuse if I need to exit halfway through this demo?*

You want to eliminate all these distracting thoughts immediately so the audience isn't doing the guesswork. To accomplish this, state some key items up front.

In my case, the very first thing I say at the beginning of each demo meeting is a clear statement presenting my number one goal for the meeting, which is for the prospect to try my product. I position my own mindset around this expectation so I'm convinced that everyone who sees my demo will want to evaluate my product. I want to set that expectation for them, because then it's more likely to happen!

Take a look at my expectation statement below. Pay attention to the wording and how it leads the audience to the outcome I intend:

> The goal today is to show you how my product can help you. My demo is going to look good—it better—because I set it up that way. <laughter> But my product really only matters if it shows value in your environment. That is why every demo turns into an eval of my product—because, of course, you're going to want to try it.

That one statement of telling the client "every demo turns into an eval" does so much to get me the desired result. So practice it! If I deliver this opening statement properly, the audience's perception instantly shifts to, *Well, if everyone goes for the free evaluation, and there's no obligation, then of course I'd like to try it out.*

Be confident with your expectation statement. Don't ask them *if* they want to try the product and evaluate it, assume they want to do a free trial period and evaluation. If you lead them, they will follow.

An extra step you can choose to implement is to say something along the lines of, "Before we end today, let's briefly talk about the eval and set a brief follow-up call to plan it. Is that okay?" And the response you'll usually get is a, "Yeah, sure. Sounds good," or at least a few nods. Those are both verbal confirmations for next steps.

You might also want to set some other expectations up front like the time frame and possibly a meeting agenda. I usually confirm the time frame at the beginning of the meeting, so everyone is aware of how much time the demo will take, including time for questions. This will put the audience at ease to at least know that they won't have to endure a one- or two-hour sales pitch.

Sometimes I even state that I have a hard stop at a certain time, and this is a great opportunity to add a little bit of personality and humor to the meeting right away. I'll say, "Isn't it great when the salesman puts a time constraint on the meeting? At least you know that I won't still be here in an hour just talking your ear off." And everyone laughs because they know that's exactly how most salespeople operate, but more importantly, they're already more engaged.

For some meetings I might build out a detailed agenda with times allocated for each topic. This can be very effective for in-depth meetings where you want to confirm what the audience wants to see and there is a lot to cover. I also like to assign time to each topic so I make sure we can get to everything.

If you want the meeting to go as desired, be thoroughly prepared, and the rest will follow!

## QUICK-HIT ACTION

 State the meeting objectives upfront
to get your desired result.

## SHOW THE BEST FIRST

Hit 'em with the WOW factor right away during a demo.

If you're using a slideshow, don't use all those frontmatter slides
introducing the history of your company, how large it is, the
current president, board of directors, and corporate headquarters. The client doesn't care! You might be offended, but
they don't even really care what your product is called or how
it's spelled. It doesn't matter to them. What they care about is if
your product can help them solve a problem they have or help
them achieve an objective. That's it!

Don't save all the "aha" moments until the end by trying to build
up dramatically towards some big reveal. Paint the picture of a
better life for them early in the demo and ride that momentum.

I've seen too many sales engineers spend the first fifteen minutes of a demo talking about the product's architecture or how to install and set up the software. Do these sound like items prospects are interested in at this point in the sales process? Probably not because they don't even know how the software is going to overcome their current dilemmas. This is why I immediately address solving their problems at the very beginning of the demo meeting. I have the most amount of attention at the beginning, so I capitalize on it by presenting a better work life for them. I hit 'em with my aha moment up front!

Before I figured this out, I wasted valuable time showing non-essentials and withheld the aha moment until the end. But I realized that I always had to wake the audience back up. When I changed my approach, however, and started showing the best first, I found that the audience always asked more engaging questions, and those questions ended up primarily leading the rest of the demo.

It's nearly impossible to keep people's interest for sixty to ninety minutes. Most standup comedians can't do this. So for a salesperson to attempt it is, well, a joke.

Even though I might have scheduled a sixty-minute demo, that doesn't mean I need to use all of that time. You just need to show them enough so they would want to try it ... that's it!

Hit them with the WOW factor
right away.

# DRAW THEM OUT

When you set the expectations and show the best first, you've already built a platform of trust with your audience by not wasting their time. On their end, they will recognize that you're not the typical salesperson who they're used to dealing with, so they'll feel the need to reciprocate the sincerity and professionalism you've shown them because you've led by example.

At this point in the meeting, quickly turn the conversation over to them by asking questions to learn more about their needs. In fact, you can build on the "how" questions you asked in the discovery call earlier and probe deeper. You want to keep them talking as much as possible in order to draw out more details and specifics about their pains and problems.

Most salespeople talk more than fifty percent of the time when they meet with a prospect. It's easy for some to talk even ninety percent of the time! This is a major pitfall. You've got to flip this dynamic and get the client talking more than you. Doing so enables you to truly understand their business operations so you can customize a solution to their exact needs. The more you do this, the more your client will realize they need your product or service. So use lots of questions to draw them out.

If you don't get them talking, they might be building up objections and reasons not to eval your product, which you won't be aware of unless you ask. Asking positions you ahead of this predicament.

Picture it as a give-and-take between you and your audience: they share a few needs they have, and then you show how your product helps with those. The more iterations you go through, the more they share and the more interested they get.

A good sign is when customers ask questions. However, keep your responses short and focused. Don't try to elaborate in three different directions for ten minutes if a twenty-second response will do. Keep it sharp! Many questions are just people wanting to be heard.

If a client asks a question that you can't answer, don't dance around it flailing for a response. Instead, you can build rapport and connection with the person by offering to follow up later with an exact and more thorough answer. This happens to me all the time. Rather than stumbling over a customer question that I don't have a solid answer to, I turn it into a potential reason to move forward with the eval. I always write down the question in my notebook, read it back to them so they know I'm paying close attention and want to understand their question, and then I respond with a customer story.

For example, I might say, "That's a great question, Customer A is very similar to you, and I'm pretty sure they overcame that same issue with my product. But I'll double check to make sure." Customers will appreciate, and even be impressed, that you pursued an answer to their question and followed up a day or two later. I've also found it effective to add in comments like, "When you try out my product, you'll see it first hand." Again, this subtly leads them into the eval! All of these small details are important and truly make a difference to achieving the next steps.

There are times when prospects ask technical questions, especially since I'm presenting software, so I'll simply answer these types of questions with, "My sales engineer will be able to answer that for you in our next meeting when we discuss the eval."

This also reminds me of an important point—I've known too many salespeople in my line of work who are afraid to do their own demo without their sales engineer simply because they don't like questions that they don't know the answer to. So if you typically operate with a partner or assistant (like a sales engineer, in my case), don't be afraid to do a demo without that person! Utilize unanswered questions to either follow up with prospects, meet with them again, or lead them into the eval.

### QUICK-HIT ACTION

Draw your customer out with preplanned questions.

You've nailed your demo and now the prospect wants to try your product. Capitalize on all the hard work you've done to get to this point by closing the deal. The last chapter will help you ensure that all of your hard work pays off.

# Chapter 9

# CONVERT
# YOUR SALE

The game is on the line. So listen up!

You've maintained control of the game this far, but how you quarterback this final play will determine whether you get the big win or the big "you gave it your best effort" speech from your coach during the bus ride home.

You just ran 15 plays, drove 85 yards down the field, and now have the ball on the one-yard line.

But there's only time to run one final play before the clock reads zero.

If you come up short, the game is lost and all of that effort will be for nothing.

Now is not the time to be unfocused or make excuses. It's the time to be hyperfocused. It's the time to scrounge up every last bit of energy you have and leave it all on the field. It's the time to step up, be a leader, and blast through that final yard and into the end zone!

You've worked hard all season for this moment. Make it count—finish strong and get the victory.

"HIKE."

What's your move?

**SWAGGER TIP:** Don't slow down when you get close to the end zone. Score the touchdown!

In sales, unfortunately, it's not enough to have just played a good game. You have to get the ball in the end zone or watch all of your hard work and effort wash down the drain. There's nothing more frustrating than focusing on a potential client for weeks and months, and then that client pumps the brakes on the entire sale at the last minute. We've all been in this situation.

I've put a lot of emphasis on tracking your metrics, being smart with your time, building a sales formula, and a few other tactical measures I believe in. However, it's easy to get enamored with activity and feel like you're doing well.

But don't confuse activity with results.

Remember the sales formula and close business. At a minimum, I was closing a deal at every other eval—which led to $500,000 in sales per month:

---

**4 Evals/mo. ➔ $500k/mo.**

---

When I was working in inside sales during the earliest part of my sales career, I was tracked on how many dials I did each day, how many total minutes I was on the phone, and how many emails I sent out. The concept was just smile and dial, smile and dial, smile and send generic email, and then twenty more generic emails. Everything tracked was just data, data, data, and more data.

On a typical day, I was hitting eighty to ninety dials per day and eighty to ninety outbound emails per day. As I mentioned in Chapter 2, there was a competitive nature to this inside sales job because the company had a giant metrics board that listed each sales rep and their numbers for each day. It was really more like a "ranking" system because the list of sales reps was in order of top metrics to bottom metrics.

I often had the highest metrics, but never the highest dollar amount in total sales. I don't think I was ever in the top ten for total sales. I wasn't naive about the metrics board. I knew that better metrics didn't put any more money in my pocket. I understood it more as a probability factor, as in the more calls and emails I complete, the better my odds are at landing a sale. However, it wasn't until I started working as a field-based salesman that I thoroughly understood that closing deals was more about being effective.

There isn't a direct correlation between being busy and being effective. So don't let all of the data entry, monitoring, and crunching numbers lead you into being a workhorse salesperson.

You have to close deals to be successful, because at the end of the day, the only number that measures your success as a salesperson—and mine, too, for that matter—is your percent closed to quota.

You have to *sell* stuff in order to be a *salesperson (that keeps his/ her job!)*. Imagine that!

Most clients aren't able to sign a business deal without having to jump through some hoops. It's a big process to get a company to make a substantial purchase, and it's very common for it to require five to eight executives to sign off in order to complete the sale. As a salesperson, you need to know how to lead this process, even push it at times, but without being pushy. It's a difficult tightrope to master, but this is the kind of swagger I'm talking about.

In my specific line of sales, a large deal legitimately takes twenty or more people to be aligned before I'm closing the deal. I usually get my foot in the door with one person, but there's still a long process ahead of me before a consensus and buying decision are made.

I've had certain accounts that took me two and a half years of prospecting and discovery calls to finally find the right person and use case. After finishing the eval, it's NOT time to kick back, ease up, and coast your way through until a decision is made. It's time to be diligent and hit all the remaining steps to ensure you reach the finish line.

The three sections below are each a critical component that I focus on to convert a sale. Like I've mentioned several times, your exact process might include a different closing cycle, but I imagine time is of the essence all the same! You'll see this point emphasized in these sections.

# CRUSH THE EVAL

Every single free trial and evaluation eventually leads to a closed deal. If you truly believe that, you will act like it. That's the swagger every salesperson needs to adopt.

There are two primary routes that lead to the beginning of the eval.

The first is when the eval begins immediately following the demo meeting. This occurs when the customers you're presenting to are excited and open to installing the software right away in order to try it out. If you have this opportunity, capitalize on their excitement and do it immediately.

I remember an instance when this exact scenario happened. I did a quick, twenty-minute demo and really dug into a current problem this client had that my product could solve right away. So at the end of the demo I said, "Why don't we just try my product now." The prospect looked at me a little star struck, but I didn't say a word; I kept my mouth shut. After an awkward pause, the prospect said, "Well, how would we do that?" I told him we could go to his computer, download the software in a few minutes, and start it up. He was a little reluctant, but I said, "What have you got to lose?" I then followed with, "There's a good chance my software resolves your problem instantly like it has for other customers." He got up and motioned for me to follow him to his work cubicle.

I walked him through the install process, and a few minutes later, he was impressed ... very impressed. He stood up to peek above his cubicle and called to a few of his colleagues, saying, "Hey! Come check this out!" And two more employees came to see what all the hype was about and ended up just as excited and loving my product.

The second route is when the demo meeting went well, but more discussions or meetings need to occur before the company is willing or allowed to dive into the eval. This is not a bad scenario to be in! When you schedule the follow-up meeting, call it an "eval planning meeting" so everyone understands the projected outcome.

An eval planning meeting is essentially a strategy meeting for those customers who are all about the logistics of everything. So give them the logistics thoroughly and professionally.

At some point, you'll want to establish what I call "eval success criteria." This is essentially a way for you to clearly show each prospect that your product met or exceeded their expectations. In order for this to work best, you need to create this criteria in collaboration with the prospect or members of the company. Their participation is key because you want them to determine their own expectations!

I create eval success criteria in a workshop-style for each prospect. I provide a list of common expectations from other clients to use as an example, and then proceed with asking the prospects about their own expectations, requirements, and what they want to prove out in the eval process.

I ask—they answer—I type!

When possible, I remind them of their pains so I can showcase value by solving them. It's in my best interest to drive the requirements in my favor. I want them to select requirements that I know my product can do, but the competition can't.

We agree on four to seven requirements and move forward from there.

I make it known that the eval process will help prove these items out and that I'll provide an analysis on each item listed in a wrap-up presentation. I'll talk more on this analysis and presentation in the next section, but for now, just note that you want to use this criteria to show value quickly, and document it each time you see this occurring.

You want the eval process to be tight, brief, and goal oriented.

So set up a timeline to outline everything, like scheduled check-ins and any other follow-up meetings. Don't plan to just reach out casually and randomly with emails that say things like, "Just wanted to see how everything is going" or "I'm here if you need anything." You certainly don't want to rush the customer or pressure them to the point where they start second-guessing you as a salesperson, but you do want to drive the impression of timeliness.

You've already made the customer a priority and have been diligent to their requests and needs, so set up the expectation of a short, efficient eval process and they'll more than likely follow your lead.

## QUICK-HIT ACTION

 Get the technical win by meeting
their success criteria...fast!

# BUILD THE
# BUSINESS CASE

Your prospect's company has operated without your product or service thus far, so why do they need your solutions? A business case is an analysis and justification that answers "why."

Remember that your offering costs money, so upper management will want to know about the cost analysis, return on investment (ROI), and other specs to help them make their decision. These numbers should be presented within the business case you put together in order to "wow!" your prospect and leave them without any objections.

Don't wait until the eval is over before you start building the business case. Their excitement is at its highest during the eval, so you want to expedite the buying process and keep the momentum going.

Do you know why I start building the business case on day one of the eval, sometimes even before the eval process begins? Because I have the swagger to trust myself that every single eval will (eventually) convert to a sale. I'm not waiting for the customer to tell me when they are done with the eval, and when they are ready to buy. I act with swagger, because I know they have needs and pains that my product can solve. When we start proving that to them, I assume the sale. I know they will buy and they follow my lead. Too many salespeople wait for the customer to lead them.

So what should the business case include?

- The problems they have without your product

- Why they need your product

- Life with your product vs. without your product

- ROI hypothesis

- Why change now?

I like to make the business case short and sweet. It should be simple; complexity causes confusion, and as some say "analysis paralysis." Simplicity gives them the belief they can implement and get the desired value they want.

Every interaction I have with them, I'm taking notes for usage in the business case.

While I'm building the business case, I'm showing different stakeholders the business case in progress. I'm getting their input on certain parts of it and asking them if they have any other thoughts they'd like to speak to on a specific topic. Not only does this help me add more content to the business case, but the more involved everyone is in building it, the more invested everyone is in it because they helped build it themselves. When they see their input and thoughts reflected on the slides, that's HUGE! They're fully on board with closing the deal at that point.

Don't try to build the business case with just one or two of your foot-in-the-door contacts. Include a lot of team members' input in order to build a consensus within the company.

The management team is going to trust the voices of the core employees who will benefit from this product over a salesperson. The company has salespeople telling them they need all kinds of products/services all the time, so it doesn't hold as much weight coming from you, the salesperson.

The key is often that you have to lead them through this process. Your sponsors are not in sales. If they were, they'd have your job—so you have to lead them through the whole process. On the bright side, this allows you the posture of being in control of setting up the expectations and then driving them home for the win.

All of the work that goes into building the business case is in anticipation of a "finale" meeting with the management and key decision-making team that results in a commitment to move forward with purchase.

## QUICK-HIT ACTION

Start the business case early and lead your client through the process.

# CLOSE THE DEAL

If you want to stumble into the biggest pitfall of your sales career, take a backseat by saying something like, "I'll give you some time to think through everything" or "Get in touch with me when you're ready."

These types of statements are dangerous because when you're selling anything, the biggest competitor is "do nothing" or keeping the status quo. This means the client continues to do things the way they've always done, without my product. Life would be better with my product, but that requires change, and people resist change.

Every company has its decision makers, but usually there is one key person who gets the job done, no matter what the job is. A great read called *The Challenger Sale* by Matthew Dixon and Brent Adamson discusses this concept in depth and coined this individual as the "mobilizer." In short, the mobilizer is your champion because he or she has a respected level of influence within their company that could potentially make or break this sale for you.

Your goal as the salesperson is to figure out who your mobilizer is during the demo and eval process. This is the person who is going to work in your favor to make something happen and who will eventually help you push the deal through.

There will be cases when your mobilizer isn't necessarily a decision maker, but rather someone who has significant influence towards the decision makers and the decision-making process. This type of scenario is common and typically doesn't have a positive or negative effect, as far as I'm concerned. No matter who your mobilizer is within the company, as long as they understand the value of your product and the value of you as a salesperson, you'll be in good hands.

A brief side note, if you've made a friend with your mobilizer and can tell that he or she likes you, lean into this role! Still focus on value first, but remember, people like to buy things from people they like.

Since I sell software, the prospects I usually get my foot in the door with are tech personnel, but these aren't the decision makers. Even if they're in control of the technical side of a business and love my product, it's still unlikely that they own a budget or are involved in the company's expansion plans. I therefore need to present my product as part of a strategic objective for a company, or it's not going to get any funding.

Make sure you are being both active and influential throughout the eval, business case, and while closing the deal. However, don't latch onto your mobilizer to the point where they're your only point of contact. Get high and wide within the company's personnel.

Getting wide means talking to a variety of people, not just a few. This is important because big company purchases often require twenty to thirty people in alignment before a deal can move forward. Getting high in the company means introducing yourself to high-level decision makers, like directors, VPs and CxOs.

If you are in excellent standing with other, current clients, try to set up a reference call between the two parties. No matter how genuine you are or how much value you've already displayed, you're still a salesperson, so a reference call between a prospect and a current customer holds more weight than the salesperson telling them how great the product is.

I've said it once but I'll say it again: you have reciprocity working for you at this point, so use it! Don't feel bad or weird for getting personal with the client and telling them what you need from them, because you've already given them a significant amount of your time and attention. Here's a simple way to navigate reciprocity vs. being pushy: let the client know that your executive management team is excited and is on standby waiting to hear from you (the salesperson) about the final, closing details.

Knowing how to leverage reciprocity without being too pushy is next-level swagger for a salesperson.

Closing a deal can be a complex process with price quotes and completing contracts between your company and theirs. It can be a frustrating process but be diligent because enthusiasm dwindles quickly if a week or two turns into a few months of internal meetings to discuss everything. The more time that passes, the more likely clients are to go dark—remember this. Time kills deals—so act with urgency.

## QUICK-HIT ACTION

 Get high and wide in the company
to build consensus...
and score the touchdown!

You've put in a lot of work...and have finally made it to the end...almost! Follow and master the actions outlined in this chapter to close the deal and get the big win. However, don't define yourself from a single game—a.k.a a single sales cycle. Don't let a win distract you, and don't let a loss drag you down. You're a pro, so you have a lot of important games ahead of you to look forward to. You need to stay sharp! I've written the Conclusion section as a challenge to help you do just that...stay sharp!

# Conclusion

I brought up Michael Jordan in the introduction and mentioned that people noticed the way he carried himself. He would arrive at a different team's arena, step onto their court, and know that he was about to get the win. He radiated confidence on and off the court. However, Michael Jordan didn't win six NBA championships because he had swagger. He won six NBA championships because he put in the work. His swagger slowly built up because he put in the work and was relentless about success.

You have to put in the work to be successful in sales.

The most difficult part is knowing *what* to do, and I've come across this time and time again when working with new salespeople at my company. If you don't know what to do, then working in sales can be a real drag. But if you do know what to do, then working in sales can be like magic. Quite literally, it can be life changing because of the financial independence and stability you can establish in a much shorter amount of time compared to most professions.

I wrote this book because I figured out *what* to do. It took me years to figure out everything that I've just shared with you! But I also figured that there's no reason for other salespeople to grind through the trial and error process like I had to. The tips in this book worked for me—but they've also worked for other salespeople that I've mentored. So I wrote this book because I wanted to keep helping even more salespeople fast track their way to success.

What you've learned in this book is not theoretical concepts. I intentionally wrote this book as a practical, actionable manual or handbook where everything is within your reach— everything can easily be learned and adopted into your own sales practice. But I've said it once and I'll say it again—it takes work to sell with swagger.

So don't be an average Joe about it! And just in case I need to call you a few more names to get you fired up...

Don't be a wimp about it. Don't be a crybaby about it. Don't be a failure because you decided not to put in the work.

Don't read this book and think something like, "Oh cool" or, "Well, that was good stuff," and then go back to your same 'ole routine of not achieving your quota. You have all of the tools right here to be exceptionally successful in sales—but you'll squander the time and effort you've already spent reading this book if you don't apply what you've learned.

It only takes twenty-one days to build a habit (according to science). If you start implementing the Swagger Tips and Quick-Hit Actions that you've learned in this book, they'll be part of your routine in just three weeks (again, this is scientifically proven).

Thus, my challenge to you is to *really* give these tips and action items a shot—build them into your daily mantra. I've even decided to compile all of the Swagger Tips and Quick-Hit Actions into the following table so you can reference them all together. Use this table to springboard your success in sales:

## Your Quick-Hit Reference Guide to Selling with Swagger

| CHAPTER 1 | FUEL YOUR FIRE |
|---|---|
| Swagger Tip | Identify and master the basics of your job. |
| Quick-Hit Action 01 | Determine a future state or goal that motivates you every day. |
| Quick-Hit Action 02 | Dedicate fifteen minutes of your day to self-improvement. |
| Quick-Hit Action 03 | Add creative humor to your workday and client interactions. |
| **CHAPTER 2** | **MAXIMIZE YOUR OUTPUT** |
| Swagger Tip | Treat yourself like a million-dollar salesperson and you'll become one. |
| Quick-Hit Action 04 | Prioritize exercise in your schedule every day. |
| Quick-Hit Action 05 | Eliminate all distractions when you work on important tasks. |
| Quick-Hit Action 06 | Begin each morning with a focus session to find your flow. |
| **CHAPTER 3** | **REGIMENT YOUR TIME** |
| Swagger Tip | Be intentional about your day by managing your time well. |
| Quick-Hit Action 07 | End each day with fifteen to thirty minutes of planning for the next day. |
| Quick-Hit Action 08 | Manage a task list to prioritize your objectives. |
| Quick-Hit Action 09 | Don't let your workday schedule you—schedule every thirty minutes and crush each segment. |
| **CHAPTER 4** | **SHARPEN YOUR SALESPERSONA** |
| Swagger Tip | Be aware of your salespersona and the impression you make on others. |
| Quick-Hit Action 10 | Establish rapport quickly by making a friend first. |
| Quick-Hit Action 11 | Develop "how" questions that will uncover pains and problems. |
| Quick-Hit Action 12 | Memorize and utilize your customer success stories. |
| **CHAPTER 5** | **NAVIGATE YOUR METRICS** |
| Swagger Tip | Don't shoot arrows into the abyss. Always aim for a target. |
| Quick-Hit Action 13 | Identify the one key metric you have 100 percent control over. |
| Quick-Hit Action 14 | Build your formula—then measure and track your activity. |
| Quick-Hit Action 15 | Build a Top 10 Opportunity List and go whale hunting! |

| CHAPTER 6 | ENHANCE YOUR PROSPECTING |
|---|---|
| Swagger Tip | Be strategic with your prospection to improve your connection rate. |
| Quick-Hit Action 16 | Offer value to achieve higher response rates. |
| Quick-Hit Action 17 | Hold yourself accountable to sending a targeted email every thirty minutes. |
| Quick-Hit Action 18 | Be persistent and creative with your follow-ups. |
| **CHAPTER 7** | **MASTER YOUR DISCOVERY CALL** |
| Swagger Tip | Ask strategic questions to keep the ball in your opponent's court to get the big win. |
| Quick-Hit Action 19 | Prepare! Prepare! Prepare! |
| Quick-Hit Action 20 | Record, rehearse, and memorize your value statement. |
| Quick-Hit Action 21 | Book yourself solid with BAMFAM! |
| **CHAPTER 8** | **NAIL YOUR DEMO** |
| Swagger Tip | Lean into the *see–try it–buy it!* mindset and see how your sales increase. |
| Quick-Hit Action 22 | State the meeting objectives up front to get your desired result. |
| Quick-Hit Action 23 | Hit them with the WOW factor right away. |
| Quick-Hit Action 24 | Draw your customer out with pre-planned questions. |
| **CHAPTER 9** | **CONVERT YOUR SALE** |
| Swagger Tip | Don't slow down when you get close to the end zone. Score the touchdown! |
| Quick-Hit Action 25 | Get the technical win by meeting their success criteria...fast! |
| Quick-Hit Action 26 | Start the business case early and lead your client through the process. |
| Quick-Hit Action 27 | Get high and wide in the company to build consensus...and score the touchdown! |

I'll add just one final proposition in my challenge to you. Revisit this book three months from now and just reread the Swagger Tips and Quick-Hit Actions. Revisit this book six months and do the same thing—and then again a year from now. Just keep revisiting this book and rereading the Swagger Tips and Quick-Hit Actions over and over and over again. And each time, when you do, ask yourself: *Have I mastered this tip?* If not, go back to that chapter or section or reread it! You purchased this book because you wanted to sell with swagger, right? This is how you do it.

Success is within your reach!

I'm grateful that you've made it all the way through this book. Thank you. There's one final bonus I'd like to give you for sticking with me all the way through, even into the conclusion!

Here's your final Swagger Tip:

**SWAGGER TIP 10:** Invest in a nice pair of sunglasses...there's nothing wrong with being stylish while you sell with swagger!

And here's your final Quick-Hit Action to take:

Set a reminder to revisit this book
and continually improve
your swagger!

Enjoy selling with swagger,

*—Tim*

CPSIA information can be obtained
at www.ICGtesting.com
Printed in the USA
BVHW041119020822
643613BV00014B/500/J